SCIENCE EXPERIMENTS

EARTH SCIENCE

BY
TAMMY K. WILLIAMS

COPYRIGHT © 1995 Mark Twain Media, Inc.

ISBN 1-58037-013-6

Printing No. CD–1816

Mark Twain Media, Inc., Publishers
Distributed by Carson-Dellosa Publishing Company, Inc.

CONTENTS

LABORATORY SKILLS 1
- Index and Materials List 1
- Classification 2
- Dichotomous Key 5
- Metric Measurement (Length) 8
- Metric Measurement (Volume) 10
- Metric Measurement (Mass/Weight) 12
- Making a Hypothesis 15
- Scientific Method: Shape of Water Splatter Versus Drop Height 18
- Scientific Method: Drop Height Versus Bounce Height 21
- Scientific Method: Rocket Engines and Newton's Third Law 24
- Lab Techniques Good Enough to Eat 27
- Answer Keys 29

GEOLOGY 31
- Index and Materials List 31
- Geologic Time Tape 32
- Heating/Cooling and Crystallization 34
- Gases in Magma 36
- Pile It On! 38
- What is the Mantle Like? 40
- Characteristics of the Earth 42
- Convection and Magma 44
- Volcano Type and Location 46
- Locating Earthquake Epicenters 49
- Identifying Rocks and Minerals 53
- If the Earth Were a Cookie 56
- Answer Keys 58

OCEANOGRAPHY 61
- Index and Materials List 61
- Water: The Mickey Mouse Molecule 63
- Water Activities 65
- Surface Tension 67
- Rock Bottom 69
- Density of Solutions 71
- Salinity of Solutions 73
- Salty Situations 75
- Salinity Testing 77
- Davey Jones's Locker 80
- Heat Capacity of Sand and Water 82
- Surface Currents 84
- Water Cycle Tales 88
- Answer Keys 89

METEOROLOGY **91**

   Index and Materials List 91

   Percent of Oxygen in Air 92

   The Pressure Is On 94

   Under Pressure 96

   Radiation and Heat Absorption (Indoors) 98

   Radiation and Heat Absorption (Outdoors) 100

   The Coriolis Effect 102

   Measuring Dew Point 104

   Weather Makers 106

   Windchill Factor 108

   Relative Humidity and Heat Index 111

   Hot Air Balloons 114

   Answer Keys 117

ASTRONOMY **119**

   Index and Materials List 119

   Planetary Motion 120

   Light Years and Student Minutes 123

   How Close Is Too Close? 124

   Estimating the Distances of Faraway Objects 125

   Estimating the Altitude of Objects 127

   Estimating the Angle of Separation of Faraway Objects 129

   Reasons for the Seasons 133

   The Greenhouse Effect 135

   Gravity and Orbital Velocity of Planets 137

   Rocket Engines and Newton's Third Law 24

   Answer Keys 139

INTRODUCTION

The processes that have shaped the earth become visible as mountain ranges, volcanoes, rocks, and trenches on the ocean floor. Those same features are affected by the water that flows over them. That water falls onto the surface of the earth, flows down the mountains and across the land, shaping the contours of the land until it pools in lakes and oceans and evaporates back into the atmosphere. Conditions in the atmosphere are in turn affected by forces present in the space surrounding Earth.

The connections between the earth, the water on its surface, the atmosphere, and the effects of extraterrestrial forces have provided the topics covered in this activity book, which contains units on geology, oceanography, meteorology, and astronomy. A unit to review and strengthen laboratory skills is also included.

In the laboratory skills section, objects are classified by different appearances, household items are given nonsense names after their characteristics are observed, experiments are conducted to measure water droplet splatter size and ball bounce height, balloon rockets are constructed, and finally, an edible test of measurement skills is conducted.

In the geology unit, layers of the "earth" are deposited, folded, then eaten; the mantle of the earth is "mixed up," poured through fingers, and rolled into a ball; and riches are mined from the "earth" and then eaten. The crystallization of rocks is modeled, the circulation of material underground is observed, and earthquake epicenters are plotted.

In the oceanography section, "water molecules" are built, cups full of water are filled with pennies until they spill, an "ocean" has its bottom mapped, and mystery solutions are "stacked" in straws according to densities and the amount of salt that each contains.

In the meteorology section, the percent of oxygen in the air is calculated, aluminum cans are crushed by the air pressure in the room, hail is created in test tubes, and hot air balloons are built and flown.

Finally, in the astronomy section, a unit of time called a "student minute" is invented to model light years, the effects of a "mini-atmosphere" are investigated, and objects nearby have their distances away, altitudes, and angles of separation estimated in the same way that ancient astronomers used to gather information about celestial bodies.

Though each section explores very different, often unrelated topics, there are some concepts that thread their way throughout the entire book. The convection current that circulates molten magma underground causes warm water to rise and cold water to sink and is responsible for those cooling breezes that blow off the water at the beach in the summer, helping to cool the earth that is affected by heat radiated from the Sun. Enjoy the activities, and don't be afraid to get your hands dirty.

> "You learn to do what you do and not something else."
>
> Gerald Unks, Ed 41, UNC-CH, 1984

LABORATORY SKILLS INDEX AND MATERIALS LIST

CLASSIFICATION 2

Envelope containing marked colored cards of the following (or similar) designs:

large blue square, black outline, blue "A2" on it

small blue square, black outline, blue "B1" on it underlined in blue

large red circle, black outline, black "B2" on it underlined in black

small red circle, black outline, black "A1" on it

large yellow rectangle, no outline, blue "B1" on it

small yellow rectangle, no outline

DICHOTOMOUS KEY 5

Wooden snappy clothespin, sharp pencil, unsharpened pencil, wire hanger, metal fork, metal knife, metal spoon, metal nut, bolt, nickel, penny, small paper clip, large paper clip, brass fastener, black bobby pin, white button, white chalk, microwave plate, white plastic fork, white plastic knife, white plastic spoon, white odd-shaped candle (birthday number candle, etc.), white soap, colored plastic hanger, colored milk jug lid, colored two-hole button, colored four-hole button, glass jar, yellow chalk, colored soap (not yellow)

METRIC MEASUREMENT (LENGTH) 8

Items may be changed to suit your room. See pages 8–9. Meterstick required.

METRIC MEASUREMENT (VOLUME) 10

Graduated cylinder and water needed, plus nail, screw, penny, and rock that will fit in the cylinder and displace water.

METRIC MEASUREMENT (MASS/WEIGHT) 12

Triple-beam balance, items in chart on page 13, pencil sharpener, sponge, cup, and access to water.

MAKING A HYPOTHESIS 15

Test tube, chemical thermometer, sodium hydroxide (labeled "Chemical A"), baking soda (labeled "Chemical B"), vinegar, and water.

SCIENTIFIC METHOD: SHAPE OF WATER SPLATTER VERSUS DROP HEIGHT 18

Meterstick, dropper, metric ruler, water, food coloring, splatter paper.

SCIENTIFIC METHOD: DROP HEIGHT VERSUS BOUNCE HEIGHT 21

Meterstick and three different balls.

SCIENTIFIC METHOD: ROCKET ENGINES AND NEWTON'S THIRD LAW 24

Meterstick, fishing line (4–6 meters), drinking straw, tape, and balloons.

LAB TECHNIQUES GOOD ENOUGH TO EAT 27

One-gallon ziplock bag, one-quart ziplock bag, ice, vanilla, sugar, rock salt, milk. Calculate amounts necessary by multiplying recipe on page 27 by number of students.

ANSWER KEYS 29

CLASSIFICATION

Date: _____ Names: _____

INTRODUCTION: How do scientists decide that crocodiles belong in one family of organisms while alligators belong in another family?

OBJECTIVE: In science, organisms are grouped according to their different or similar characteristics. This process, called classification, allows for the study of the similarities and differences between organisms. In this activity, we will practice classifying a set of colored and marked cards in order to examine the flexibility that exists when classifying things.

PROCEDURE:
1. A set of marked colored cards are in the envelope provided.
2. Your goal is to design as many classifications systems for those cards as possible.
3. As you decide on a classification system:
   a. Arrange the cards into the system.
   b. In the chart below, identify CATEGORIES and MEMBERS in the spaces provided. Members may be drawn in or described.
   c. Draw vertical lines in the charts to separate categories.
   d. List all the members of a category in the column below the category name.

Example: SYSTEM 1: Classify by shape _____   SYSTEM 2: _____

CATEGORIES

square	circle	rectangle

MEMBERS

| A2 | B2 | |
| B1 | A1 | B1 |

Date: _____ Names: _____

SYSTEM 3:_____   SYSTEM 4:_____

CATEGORIES

M

E

M

B

E

R

S

SYSTEM 5:_____   SYSTEM 6:_____

CATEGORIES

M

E

M

B

E

R

S

Date: _____ Names: _____

SYSTEM 7:_____ SYSTEM 8: _____

CATEGORIES

M

E

M

B

E

R

S

QUESTIONS:

1. What characteristics about the cards did you use in order to classify them?

_____

_____

2. Does each classification system contain the same categories? Why/why not?

_____

_____

3. Do all categories contain the same members? Why/why not?_____

_____

_____

4. Do you think that each group in the class thought of the same classification systems that you did? _____

5. Do you think that each group in the class would agree on the same system as THE BEST SYSTEM? Why/why not? _____

_____

_____

6. Why then is it important for scientists to agree on a single classification system for each particular group of items/organisms? _____

_____

_____

Date: _____   Name: _____

DICHOTOMOUS KEY

INTRODUCTION: Once plants, animals, rocks, and minerals have been assigned by scientists to certain families or groups, how do you figure out their species or names? This is done by using a device called an identification key.

OBJECTIVE: In science, organisms, rocks, minerals, and elements are identified and classified according to characteristics that they possess. These characteristics may be either similar to or different from those of other organisms. When differences are observed so that the presence or absence of a characteristic determines which category the organism or object falls into, the identification tool is called a DICHOTOMOUS KEY. In this activity, we will use a dichotomous key to give household items nonsense names.

PROCEDURE: 1. For each item below, read the description and follow the directions at the end of the line.
2. When the description is followed by a nonsense name, write in the actual name of the household item on the blank line

1a. Object is partly or completely made of metal .... go to 2

1b. Object has no metal on it .... go to 16

2a. Object has nonmetal parts .... go to 3

2b. Object is completely made of metal .... go to 5

3a. Object is less than 10 cm in length .... whippersnapper _____

3b. Object is 10 cm or greater in length .... go to 4

4a. Object is pointed at one end .... tapered doodad _____

4b. Object is not pointed at one end .... common doodad _____

5a. Object is greater than 10 cm .... go to 6

5b. Object is 10 cm or less .... go to 9

6a. Object has a twisted area .... thingamajig _____

6b. Object has no twisted area .... go to 7

7a. Object has 3 or more prongs .... left-handed monkey wrench _____

7b. Object has no prongs .... go to 8

Date: _____ Names: _____

8a. Object has a cutting edge .... geegaw _____

8b. Object has no cutting edge .... scooperdoo _____

9a. Object has spiral grooves .... go to 10

9b. Object has no spiral grooves .... go to 11

10a. Object has a hole .... cashew _____

10b. Object has no hole .... whatsit _____

11a. Outside edge is a circle .... go to 12

11b. Outside edge is not a circle .... go to 13

12a. Object is silver-colored .... quinto _____

12b. Object is not silver-colored .... uno _____

13a. Object is silver-colored .... go to 14

13b. Object is not silver-colored .... go to 15

14a. Object is less than 4 cm in length .... micro whatnot _____

14b. Object is 4 cm or more in length .... macro whatnot _____

15a. Object is brass-colored .... skyhook _____

15b. Object is not brass-colored .... dingus _____

16a. Object is white .... go to 17

16b. Object is not white .... go to 24

17a. Object has holes .... wadget _____

17b. Object has no holes .... go to 18

18a. Object is a circle in at least one dimension .... go to 19

18b. Object is not a circle in any dimension .... go to 20

Date: _____ Names: _____

19a. The circumference of the circular dimension is 6 cm or less... bric-a-brac _____

19b. The circumference of the circular dimension is greater than 6 cm ....
.... roundabout _____

20a. Object is made of plastic .... go to 21

20b. Object is not made of plastic .... go to 23

21a. Object has 3 or more prongs .... doohickey _____

21b. Object has no prongs .... go to 22

22a. Object has a cutting edge .... gismo _____

22b. Object does not have a cutting edge .... flim flam _____

23a. Object appears to have a string running through its center .... wickey _____

23b. Object does not appear to have a string running through its center ....
.... scrubadub _____

24a. Object is made of plastic .... go to 25

24b. Object is not made of plastic .... go to 28

25a. Outer edge of the object is round .... go to 26

25b. Outer edge of the object is not round .... whatchamacallit _____

26a. Object has holes .... go to 27

26b. Object has no holes .... spinaroo _____

27a. Object has 2 holes .... bihole _____

27b. Object has 4 holes .... tetrahole _____

28a. Object is made of glass .... seethru _____

28b. Object is not made of glass .... go to 29

29a. Object is yellow in color .... screecher _____

29b. Object is not yellow in color .... soaky _____

Date: _____   Names: _____

METRIC MEASUREMENT (LENGTH)

INTRODUCTION: If your hand is 3 inches wide, how many centimeters wide is it? Which metric unit is closest to the length of 1 yard?

OBJECTIVE: In this activity, we will review metric units for measuring distance or length—the meter, decimeter, centimeter, and millimeter. We will also use these units to estimate and then measure the sizes of various objects around the room.

Meterstick: 1 meter (m) = 10 decimeters (dm) OR 100 centimeters (cm) OR 1,000 millimeters (mm) Here is a visual representation of a meterstick.

0   10   20   30   40   50   60   70   80   90   100 cm

0–1 is 1 centimeter   1 decimeter   ** 1 millimeter is the distance between each tiny black mark on a meterstick.

PROCEDURE: 1. Use a meterstick to measure the objects listed in the chart below. Make sure you use the metric side of the meterstick (with numbers to 100 cm, not 36 inches).
2. Measure the objects in the units listed. Write the unit abbreviation after the measurement you get (example: instead of 47.5, write 47.5 cm).

OBJECT	MEASUREMENT	UNITS
Length of your table		Meters (m)
Width of your table		Decimeters (dm)
Length of a piece of paper		Centimeters (cm)
Width/thickness of a pencil		Millimeters (mm)

3. Which unit above is closest to the following size:
a. the thickness of a fingernail?_____
b. the width of a finger? _____
c. the width of a hand? _____
d. longer than your leg? _____

Date: _____ Names: _____

4. Keep the sizes of each of the metric units in mind. For each object listed in the chart below:

   a. Choose the most appropriate unit of measurement (m, dm, cm, mm) and record that unit in the chart in the "Unit Chosen" column.

   b. Estimate the size of that object using the units you chose and the "body parts" in step 3a–d above. You may actually lay fingers side-by-side along an object to see how many centimeters long it is. Record your estimates in the chart below under the "Estimate" column.

   c. Get up and measure the objects listed using the units that you chose. Record your measurements in the chart below under the "Measurement" column. You do not have to measure the items in the order listed.

OBJECT	UNIT CHOSEN	ESTIMATE (WITH UNITS)	MEASUREMENT (WITH UNITS)
Height of table			
Length of tabletop			
Height of classroom door			
Thickness of tabletop			
Width of cabinets			
Thickness of a pencil lead			
Width of your table leg			

QUESTIONS:

1. Which unit might be best used to measure: a. shoe length? _____

b. thickness of hair strands? _____

c. a bus length? _____

d. width of a door? _____

e. length of a hallway? _____

f. height of the letter "E"? _____

g. length of a pencil? _____

2. How is the metric system more simple to use than English units (like inches, feet, and yards)?

_____

Date: _____ Names: _____

METRIC MEASUREMENT (VOLUME)

INTRODUCTION: The volume of a cube can be calculated by multiplying its length times its width times its height. How could you figure out the volume of a rock that has broken and chipped edges? How could you figure out the volume of a bag of marbles without doing a lot of math?

OBJECTIVE: In this activity, we will learn how to read the volume of a liquid in a graduated cylinder measuring milliliters (mL) by reading the meniscus of the liquid (see diagram below). When most liquids are placed in tall, narrow containers, they tend to creep up the walls of the container a little due to capillary action. This results in the surface of the liquid appearing to be curved. The bottom of this curve is known as the MENISCUS, and it best represents the actual volume of liquid in the cylinder. We will also learn how to measure the volume of odd-shaped objects.

Graduated cylinder:

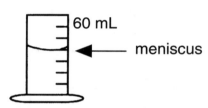

PROCEDURE:

1. Pour the colored liquid from the beaker at your lab station into the graduated cylinder.

2. Sit the graduated cylinder flat on the countertop.

3. Bend down so that the water level is at eye level and look for the meniscus.

4. Record the number of milliliters of liquid (to the nearest one-half mL) in the chart on the next page. This step will be done **before** each object is lowered into the liquid. Since this prepares us to measure the first object, record the liquid volume in the first box under "Beginning Volume" (second column).

5. Once a starting liquid volume has been measured, gently lower an object into the liquid. The amount that the water rises (amount of water displaced) is equal to the volume of the object.

6. Read the new volume at the meniscus and record it in the chart under "Volume of Liquid & Object" for that object (first column).

7. To calculate the volume of the object alone, subtract the "Beginning Volume" from the "Volume of Liquid & Object" (column 2 from column 1).

8. Repeat the above steps for each of the remaining objects.

OBJECT	VOLUME OF LIQUID & OBJECT	–	BEGINNING VOLUME (LIQUID)	=	VOLUME OF OBJECT
Nail					
Screw					
Penny					
Rock					

Date: _____ Names: _____

QUESTIONS:

1. Why is it necessary to recheck the starting volume of liquid before each object is put in?

_____

_____

_____

2. What kind of error would result if you read the liquid volume where the liquid touches the wall of the cylinder rather than at the meniscus? _____

_____

_____

_____

3. How does this "measuring volume by difference" method compare with measuring volume using math for these odd-shaped objects?

_____

_____

_____

_____

Date: _____ Names: _____

METRIC MEASUREMENT (MASS/WEIGHT)

INTRODUCTION: How can you figure out how much of your pencil gets "eaten" by a pencil sharpener each time you sharpen a pencil? How can you figure out how large a gulp of water is?

OBJECTIVE: In this activity, we will become familiar with the parts of a triple-beam balance that is used to measure mass, and we will practice measuring the mass of different objects. Following this, we will learn how to "weigh-by-difference" to find the mass of different objects.

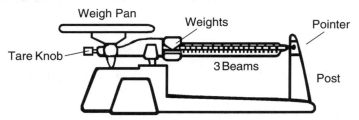

PROCEDURE: To "ZERO A BALANCE"
1. Check to make sure that the balance is clean. Wipe and clean it if necessary.

2. Move all weights to the left of the balance (next to the weigh pan).

3. Look to see if the pointer line is perfectly in line with the mark on the post. This indicates whether the balance is zeroed.

4. If the lines do not meet, adjust the TARE KNOB, which is located underneath the weigh pan, by turning it a little and observing its effect. You should be able to zero the balance by repeating this procedure.
** If you cannot zero the balance, ASK FOR ASSISTANCE!

To Weigh Objects
1. Use the following steps to weigh each object listed in the chart (in grams) and record its weight in the chart.

2. Make sure the balance is zeroed and the weigh pan is clean.

3. Place an object on the weigh pan.

4. Move the weights on the beams until the pointer just balances at the white mark on the post. Do this by first moving the small weight to the right. If it is too light to balance the object, move it back to the left (to 0) and try the next larger weight. Continue this until one of the weights can be placed so that the pointer is both above and below the post line.
** Make sure that the 2 larger weights fall into notches as you move them on the beams.

12

Date: _____ Names: _____

5. Weights can be measured as accurately as the nearest tenth of a gram by positioning the smallest weight.

6. Once the weights have been positioned so that the beam pointer aligns with the mark on the post, add each of the marked weights together to get a total. Remember, the smallest weight marks single grams, and the lines between the numbers on that beam mark tenths of grams. The medium-sized weight marks tens of grams, and the largest weight marks hundreds of grams.

7. Record the total mass in the chart below under "Weight." Write in units.

8. Store the balance clean and with all the weights on zero.

OBJECT	WEIGHT (IN GRAMS)
Small paper clip	
2 small paper clips	
Large paper clip	
2 large paper clips	
One penny	
Empty beaker	
Something you choose: _____	

To Weigh By Difference
1. When doing this, we will be weighing an object, taking away some of or adding to the object, and then reweighing the object to see how much was taken away or added.

2. First, weigh each of the objects listed in the chart on page 14. Record their weights under the column "Weight Before."

3. For each object remove or add to it by:
    a. putting the sponge in water.
    b. drinking a swallow of water from the cup.
    c. sharpening the pencil.

4. Reweigh each item after step 3 and record its new weight under "Weight After."

Date: _____ Names: _____

5. To find the amount of change (weight gained or lost) subtract the smaller number from the larger number. If the starting number is larger, the weight was lost. If the ending weight was larger, then the weight was gained.

6. Include the units as well as whether weight was gained or lost.

7. Store the balance clean and dry and with all weights on zero.

OBJECT	WEIGHT BEFORE	WEIGHT AFTER	WEIGHT CHANGE (GRAMS)
Dry sponge (put in water)			
Cup of water (take a sip)			
Pencil (sharpen)			

QUESTIONS:

1. Why is it important to make sure that the weigh pan is clean before weighing objects?

_____

_____

_____

2. How does "weighing by difference" compare to something like saving pencil shavings and weighing them to find out how much is sharpened off? _____

_____

_____

_____

_____

_____

_____

Date: _____ Names: _____

MAKING A HYPOTHESIS

INTRODUCTION: Do you know what will happen if you mix vinegar and baking soda? Will the temperature change? Will bubbles form? Guessing what will happen is called making a hypothesis.

OBJECTIVE: A hypothesis is a "best guess" because the outcome of a question is guessed using only what is known before the question is tested. The hypothesis is then tested using experiments. During the experiment, data or information is collected to check the accuracy of the hypothesis. Finally, using the results of the experiment, the hypothesis may be supported as correct or it may be changed. In this activity, we will make hypotheses about how combining liquids with two different chemicals will affect the temperature of each liquid.

PROCEDURE: <u>CHEMICAL A AND WATER</u>

1. Place your hypothesis for "Chemical A and Water" below. What do you think will happen?

[ ]

2. Measure 5 mL of water in the graduated cylinder and pour it into a test tube.
3. Place the test tube in the test tube rack and gently place the thermometer in the water in the test tube.
4. After 1 minute, record the temperature of the water and record this temperature in the chart on page 16 under "Start."
5. Using the metal spatula, add 3 pellets of "Chemical A" to your test tube. DO NOT TOUCH THE PELLETS WITH YOUR SKIN!
6. Observe and record the temperature of the water every 15 seconds for 3 minutes.
7. At the end of 3 minutes, remove the thermometer, pour the contents of the test tube down the drain, and rinse the test tube and thermometer.
8. Graph the data from the chart onto the graph sheet on the next page. Use a SOLID LINE to connect the dots of data.

<u>CHEMICAL B AND VINEGAR</u>

9. Place your hypothesis for "Chemical B and Vinegar" below. What do you think will happen?

[ ]

10. Repeat the exact procedure used for Chemical A, EXCEPT:
    a. In #2 above, begin with 5 mL of vinegar.
    b. In #5 above, add 1/2 teaspoon of "Chemical B."
11. Graph the data for Chemical B on the graph on the next page. Use a BROKEN LINE to connect the data points.

Date: _____ Names: _____

DATA:

TEMPERATURE CHANGE (DEGREES CELSIUS)

Time (seconds)

	Start	15	30	45	60	75	90	105	120	135	150	165	180
CHEMICAL A													
CHEMICAL B													

TEMPERATURE VERSUS TIME

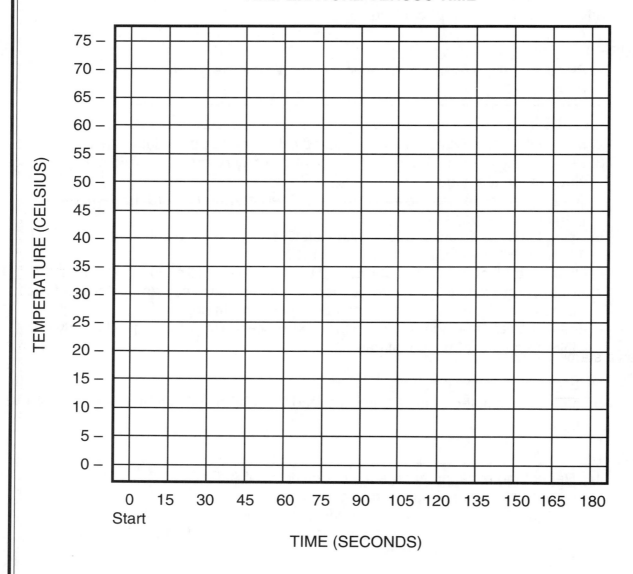

Date: _____ Names: _____

QUESTIONS:

1. What happened to the water temperature when Chemical A was added?

_____

2. What happened to the vinegar temperature when Chemical B was added?

_____

3. How did your hypothesis for Chemical A compare to your results?

_____

_____

_____

4. How did your hypothesis for Chemical B compare to your results?

_____

_____

_____

5. What do scientists need to do before accepting their hypotheses?

_____

_____

_____

6. Why was a starting temperature needed?

_____

_____

_____

7. What are the two most noticeable observations about what happens when baking soda (Chemical B) and vinegar are mixed?

_____

_____

_____

Date: _____   Names: _____

SCIENTIFIC METHOD
SHAPE OF WATER SPLATTER VERSUS DROP HEIGHT

INTRODUCTION: If you spill a liquid while you are pouring it into a glass, will it splatter more or less if you hold the pitcher two feet above the glass as opposed to four inches above?

OBJECTIVE: In this activity, we will practice using the scientific method while investigating the effect of drop height on the size and shape of water droplet splatters when they land. We will be careful to change only the one item whose effect we will observe. This is called the EXPERIMENTAL VARIABLE. All of the other conditions must be kept completely identical. These conditions are called CONTOLS.

PROCEDURE: 1. As you follow the instructions to complete the investigation below, fill in the steps of the scientific method by writing in what you do at each step in the water droplet investigation where it matches a step in the scientific method.

STATE PROBLEM: _____

_____

GATHER INFORMATION (name sources of information):

a. _____   b. _____

c. _____   d. _____

MAKE HYPOTHESIS: _____

_____

EXPERIMENT: _____

_____

_____

RECORD DATA (list examples of data): a. _____

b. _____   c. _____

FORM CONCLUSION: _____

_____

Date: _____   Names: _____

2. Add 2 drops of food coloring to your beaker.

3. Add 100 mL of water and mix.

4. Partially fill the glass dropper with colored water.

5. Measure the heights listed in the chart using a meterstick positioned with one end on the splatter paper and the other end measuring dropper height.

6. From each height, drop 3 drops of water (in different places on the paper).

7. Measure the size of the splatter in MILLIMETERS, and record each trial size in the chart. Add the sizes to get a total, and divide by 3 to find the average size of each splatter.

8. Repeat this process for each height.

9. For each drop height, write a description of the splatter in the chart, also. Examples: "Drop is very round," "Drop broke apart," or "Drop is surrounded by little splatters."

10. On the graph, plot the average splatter size versus drop height.

DATA:

DIAMETER OF DROP SPLATTERS (mm)

Drop Height	Trial 1	Trial 2	Trial 3	Total	Average	Description
5 cm						
10 cm						
20 cm						
40 cm						
80 cm						

Date: _____   Names: _____

DROP HEIGHT VERSUS SPLATTER SIZE

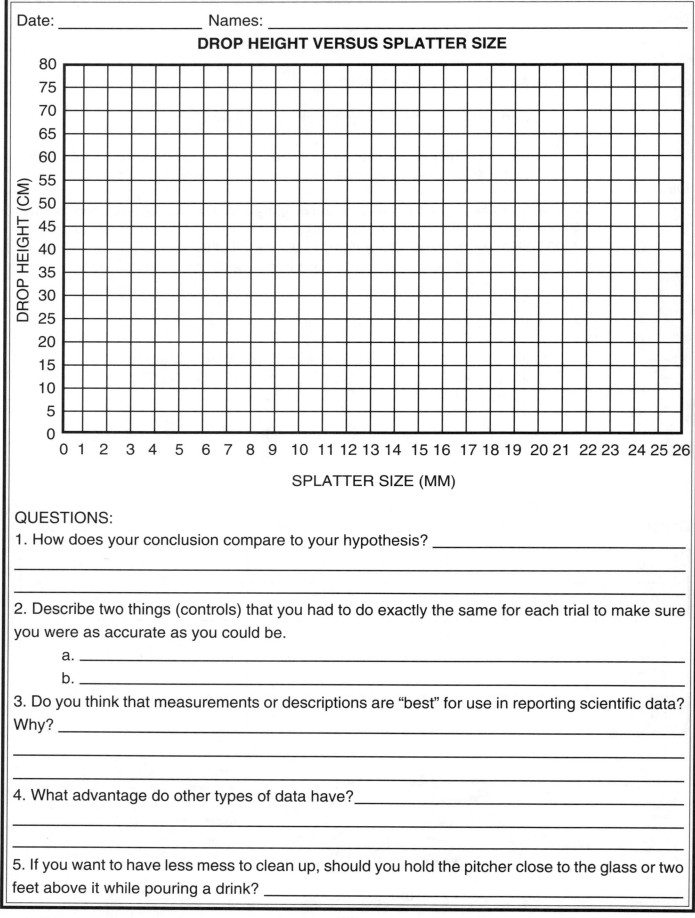

QUESTIONS:

1. How does your conclusion compare to your hypothesis? _____
_____
_____

2. Describe two things (controls) that you had to do exactly the same for each trial to make sure you were as accurate as you could be.

     a. _____

     b. _____

3. Do you think that measurements or descriptions are "best" for use in reporting scientific data? Why? _____
_____
_____

4. What advantage do other types of data have?_____
_____
_____

5. If you want to have less mess to clean up, should you hold the pitcher close to the glass or two feet above it while pouring a drink? _____

Date: _____ Names: _____

SCIENTIFIC METHOD
DROP HEIGHT VERSUS BOUNCE HEIGHT

INTRODUCTION: If you spill a toybox filled with different kinds of balls such as marbles, ping-pong balls, and rubber balls, which ball will bounce up highest? Does the height from which you spill the box of balls affect how high they bounce?

OBJECTIVE: In this activity, we will investigate how the height from which three types of objects are dropped affects their bounce heights. In conducting this investigation, we will also practice using the scientific method: conducting three trials, graphing data, and writing conclusions. We will be careful to change only the one item whose effect we will observe. This is called the EXPERIMENTAL VARIABLE. All other conditions must be kept completely identical. These conditions are called CONTROLS.

PROCEDURE:

1. As you follow the instructions to complete the investigation below, fill in the steps of the scientific method by writing what you do at each step in the drop height versus bounce height investigation.

2. STATE PROBLEM: _____

_____

_____

GATHER INFORMATION (skip this item)

3. STATE HYPOTHESIS: _____

_____

_____

4. EXPERIMENT:

a. From each of the identified heights listed in the chart, drop each of the 3 items.

b. Hold the meterstick straight up and measure the bounce height by sight. Measure the maximum height of the first bounce of the object (to the nearest centimeter), and record this height in the appropriate data chart.

c. Repeat this test twice more at each height for each item, recording the data each time.

d. When all drop heights have been tested for each object, total and average the data.

e. Graph average data on the graph provided.

Date: _____ Names: _____

5. RECORD DATA:

Item 1: _____

Drop Height	Bounce Height				
	Trial 1	Trial 2	Trial 3	Total	Average
10 cm					
20 cm					
30 cm					
40 cm					
50 cm					
60 cm					
70 cm					
80 cm					
90 cm					
100 cm					

Item 2: _____

Drop Height	Bounce Height				
	Trial 1	Trial 2	Trial 3	Total	Average
10 cm					
20 cm					
30 cm					
40 cm					
50 cm					
60 cm					
70 cm					
80 cm					
90 cm					
100 cm					

Item 3: _____

Drop Height	Bounce Height				
	Trial 1	Trial 2	Trial 3	Total	Average
10 cm					
20 cm					
30 cm					
40 cm					
50 cm					
60 cm					
70 cm					
80 cm					
90 cm					
100 cm					

Date: _____ Names: _____

6. FORM CONCLUSION: _____

_____

7. CREATE A LINE GRAPH showing the average data for each of the 3 objects.

AVERAGE DROP HEIGHT VERSUS BOUNCE HEIGHT

QUESTIONS:

1. What is the experimental variable for this experiment? _____

2. What are three controls for this experiment? a. _____

     b. _____

     c. _____

3. Which of the balls that you tested was most likely to:

     a. bounce low and stay near where it was dropped? _____

     b. bounce high and bounce away from where it was dropped? _____

Date: _____   Names: _____

SCIENTIFIC METHOD
ROCKET ENGINES AND NEWTON'S THIRD LAW

INTRODUCTION: What would happen if you stood still while wearing skates and threw baseballs away from you? Would you move? How about if you sat on a skateboard and did the same thing?

OBJECTIVE: Newton's Third Law says that for every action there is an equal and opposite reaction. This means that if you push someone away from you, you are pushed backwards with the same force that you exerted. In the same manner, if a rocket's exhaust exerts 150 newtons of force against a concrete launch pad, the same force is exerted on the rocket. This is what causes the rocket to be lifted into the air. In this activity, we will investigate this reaction using a balloon as the engine and a straw as the rocket. We will be careful to change only the one item whose effect we will observe. This is called the EXPERIMENTAL VARIABLE. All other conditions must be kept completely identical. These conditions are called CONTROLS.

PROCEDURE:
   A. STATE PROBLEM: _____

_____

   B. GATHER INFORMATION (skip this section)

   C. FORM HYPOTHESIS: _____

_____

   D. EXPERIMENT:
      1. Attach your flight string to the wall opposite from where you will stand, and pull the string out level from where it is attached. String should be 4–6 meters long.

      2. Inflate your balloon to the 3-cm diameter indicated in the chart.

      3. Hold the balloon closed or close it in some other way SO THAT IT CAN BE QUICKLY REOPENED LATER.

      4. Attach the balloon to the straw, OPEN END TOWARD YOU, CLOSED END TOWARD THE BOARD. (See diagram.)

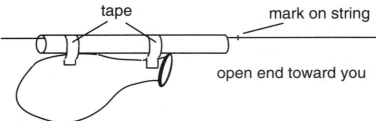

tape   mark on string

open end toward you

Date: _____ Names: _____

5. Facing the string attachment, hold the flight string level near its free end.

6. Start the straw at the mark on the string.

7. Release the rocket (balloon) and allow it to fly down the string.

8. Holding the string level, measure the distance traveled by the rocket.

9. Repeat steps 1–8 twice more for this diameter and record the data in the chart.

10. Repeat entire procedure for each diameter in the chart.

11. Graph average distances versus balloon diameter on a computer. Attach your graph printout to the lab sheet. If you don't have access to a computer, use the graph provided on page 26.

E. RECORD DATA:

Diameter of Balloon   **Distance Traveled by Balloon**

	Trial 1	Trial 2	Trial 3	Total	Average
3 cm					
6 cm					
9 cm					
12 cm					
15 cm					

F. FORM CONCLUSION: _____

_____

_____

_____

Date: _____ Names: _____

QUESTIONS:

1. What is the experimental variable in this experiment? _____

_____

2. Name three controls for this experiment:

    a. _____

    b. _____

    c. _____

3. How would Newton's Third Law affect you if you threw baseballs away from you while standing

on skates or sitting on a skateboard? _____

_____

_____

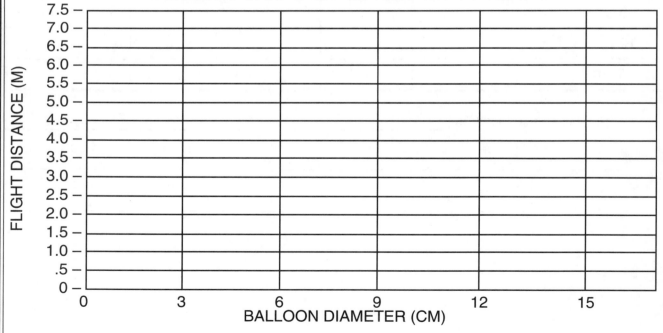

BALLOON DIAMETER VERSUS FLIGHT DISTANCE

Date: _____ Names: _____

LAB TECHNIQUES GOOD ENOUGH TO EAT

INTRODUCTION: How is cooking similar to chemistry? Both involve following directions well enough to avoid catastrophe!

OBJECTIVE: In this activity, we will practice measuring length, mass, and volume using metric units. The end product will be an indicator of your ability to measure accurately. If your measurement skills are very good, your result will be good enough to eat!

PROCEDURE:

1. Measure 16 cm from the bottom of the large plastic bag and use the pen at your lab station to mark the height.

2. Fill the bag to the line that you marked with ice (from the cooler).

3. MEASURE out 100 mL of ROCK SALT, and pour it over the ice in the large bag.

4. Take a new, small plastic bag and mix the following ingredients into this bag:
   a. 100 mL MILK
   b. 20 mL SUGAR
   c. 2 drops of VANILLA EXTRACT

5. Seal the contents of the small bag (make sure the bag is "ziplocked").

6. Place the small bag inside the large bag of ice.

7. Seal the large bag (with the small bag inside). Make sure the bag is "ziplocked."

8. Move the ice in the large bag around so that it surrounds/covers/supports the small bag.

9. Time 1-minute intervals. At the end of each 1-minute interval, turn the bag over onto the other side. (Arrange ice cubes so that they surround the small bag inside.)

10. Repeat the 1-minute "flippings" a total of 10 times.

11. At the end of the tenth minute (10 1-minute flips), time 30-second intervals and flip the bag every 30 seconds for 5 minutes (10 30-second flips).

12. At the end of the 20 flips (10 flips 1 minute apart and 10 flips 30 seconds apart), ask your instructor to check to see if your solution has completed its reaction.

Date: _____ Names: _____

13. A. You may eat your solution after it is approved . . . IF YOU DARE!
    B. If your solution is not approved, continue flipping every 30 seconds for an additional 5 minutes. Then you may complete step 13A.

** THIS MAY ALSO BE DONE WITH A BABY FOOD JAR INSIDE A COFFEE CAN WITH A PLASTIC RECLOSEABLE LID. IN THIS SET-UP, ALTERNATE HANDFULS OF ICE AND SALT AND THEN ROLL CAN UNDER FOOT.

Flip Checklist (X out numbers as you flip)

1-MINUTE FLIPS	1	2	3	4	5	6	7	8	9	10
30-SECOND FLIPS	1	2	3	4	5	6	7	8	9	10

QUESTIONS:

1. What solution do you end up with? _____

2. Instead of an explosion, what might result if you measure inaccurately?

_____

_____

_____

3. Besides successful science experiments, list two other areas where good measurement skills are important.

    a. _____

    b. _____

LABORATORY SKILLS ANSWER KEYS

CLASSIFICATION (page 4)
1. Answers will vary, but will include color, size, print color, letters or numbers on them, and so on.
2. No. The system determines what categories will be necessary.
3. No. Category members are determined by the system used.
4. Not exactly, but there will be a lot of overlap because some systems are easy to figure out.
5. No. Different people will prefer different characteristics.
6. Scientists should agree on a best system because it lessens confusion when trying to organize data.

DICHOTOMOUS KEY (pages 5–7)
3a. wooden snappy clothespin; 4a. sharp pencil; 4b. unsharpened pencil; 6a. wire hanger; 7a. metal fork; 8a. metal knife; 8b. metal spoon; 10a. metal nut; 10b. bolt; 12a. nickel; 12b. penny; 14a. small paper clip; 14b. large paper clip; 15a. brass fastener; 15b. black bobby pin; 17a. white button; 19a. white chalk; 19b. microwave plate; 21a. white plastic fork; 22a. white plastic knife; 22b. white plastic spoon; 23a. white candle; 23b. white soap; 25b. colored plastic hanger; 26b. colored milk lid; 27a. colored 2-hole button; 27b. colored 4-hole button; 28a. glass jar; 29a. yellow chalk; 29b. colored soap

METRIC MEASUREMENT (LENGTH) (pages 8–9)
3a. millimeter
  b. centimeter
  c. decimeter
  d. meter
1. Some range of error should be allowed for answers given.
  a. dm/cm
  b. mm
  c. m
  d. dm
  e. m
  f. mm
  g. cm/dm
2. The metric system is based on units of 10 so you can change from one unit to another simply by dividing or multiplying by 10. In the English system, you have to use 3, 12, 36, and so on.

METRIC MEASUREMENT (VOLUME) (page 11)
1. Water is removed with the object in each trial so the starting volume decreases and may result in a larger end volume being recorded if a new starting volume is not recorded.
2. The volume would be read higher than it actually is.
3. "Measuring by difference" is a lot easier than trying to calculate the volume using math.

METRIC MEASUREMENT (MASS/WEIGHT) (page 14)
1. A dirty weigh pan means you are weighing dirt and the starting weight is read higher than it should be.
2. "Weighing by difference" is easier than saving shavings (that blow away and stick to stuff).

MAKING A HYPOTHESIS (page 17)

1. The temperature increased.
2. The temperature decreased.
3. Will be determined by hypothesis. Hypothesis will be supported or will not be supported by data.
4. Same as #3.
5. Scientists must test their hypotheses.
6. Without a starting temperature, you won't know if the temperature increases or decreases.
7. Answers may vary, but will probably include: "The solution bubbles over, and the temperature drops."

SCIENTIFIC METHOD: SHAPE OF WATER SPLATTER VERSUS DROP HEIGHT (page 20)

1. Will be determined by hypothesis. Data will either support or not support the hypothesis.
2a. meterstick had to be held exactly straight up;
 b. you had to measure from same point on dropper each time; other controls are acceptable.
3. Measurements are probably best because they can be replicated exactly by different scientists.
4. Other data, like descriptions, give information that measurements do not (like shape).
5. Pour liquid from the closest distance to avoid the most mess.

SCIENTIFIC METHOD: DROP HEIGHT VERSUS BOUNCE HEIGHT (page 23)

1. Drop height
2a. meter stick was held perfectly upright;
 b. measurement was made from bottom of each ball;
 c. drop was made onto same surface each time
3a. lowest bouncing ball (determined by items used and data recorded)
 b. highest bouncing ball (determined by items used and data recorded)

SCIENTIFIC METHOD: ROCKET ENGINES AND NEWTON'S THIRD LAW (page 26)

1. Balloon diameter
2a. measuring from same end of straw each time;
 b. holding string perfectly level each time;
 c. not allowing rocket to move until measurement is complete each time
3. When you have no friction holding you in place, throwing objects one direction will push you in the opposite direction.

LAB TECHNIQUES GOOD ENOUGH TO EAT (page 28)

1. Ice cream
2. Bad-tasting ice cream would result.
3a. following a recipe when cooking;
 b. cutting out pieces of a pattern/puzzle; other items may be accepted.

GEOLOGY INDEX AND MATERIALS LIST

GEOLOGIC TIME TAPE **32**
> Hole puncher, construction paper, colored pencils, string, tape, meterstick, scissors, and register tape.

HEATING/COOLING AND CRYSTALLIZATION **34**
> Aluminum pan, salt water, dropper, small candle, and short beaker.

GASES IN MAGMA **36**
> Baking soda, water, mothballs, vinegar, large beaker, Alka-Seltzer tablets, popcorn kernels, spaghetti, and a teaspoon.

PILE IT ON! **38**
> Plastic knife, paper plate, white bread, wheat bread, chunky peanut butter, and jelly.

WHAT IS THE MANTLE LIKE? **40**
> Cornstarch, water, teaspoon, graduated cylinder, cup, metal stirring rod, and containers or buckets for clean-up.

CHARACTERISTICS OF THE EARTH **42**
> Silly Putty container, softball, globe, hard-boiled egg, and markers.

CONVECTION AND MAGMA **44**
> Food coloring, small bottle, 400-mL beaker, hot water, cold water, clear plastic (house plant drain) pan, four cups, and a dropper.

VOLCANO TYPE AND LOCATION **46**
> Blank world map with longitude and latitude lines.

LOCATING EARTHQUAKE EPICENTERS **49**
> Compass, maps (provided with activity), and charts of S- and P-wave relationships (provided with activity).

IDENTIFYING ROCKS AND MINERALS **53**
> Penny, glass slide, piece of metal (spatula), ceramic tile (with at least one unglazed side), marble, slate, granite, limestone, obsidian, feldspar, galena, graphite, talc, and muscovite mica are needed. Other rocks/minerals can be used by omitting the "Rock and Mineral Key" and simply having students identify characteristics.

IF THE EARTH WERE A COOKIE **56**
> Soft and hard chocolate chip cookies, toothpicks, and paper towels.

ANSWER KEYS **58**

Date: _____ Names: _____

GEOLOGIC TIME TAPE

INTRODUCTION: If you had to place the important events of your life on a time line and you could only use 1 meter of paper, what scale would you need to use to fit your life span on the time line?

OBJECTIVE: In this activity, you will construct a geologic time line that will show major geologic eras, periods, epochs, and organisms that were alive at each time so that you will get an idea of what some scientists believe is the length of each era and period, as well as how long ago each occurred according to those scientists.

****USEFUL INFORMATION ABOUT GEOLOGIC TIME IS ON THE NEXT PAGE****

PROCEDURE:

1. You need to designate the following roles for this activity:
    a. Measurer: measures the tape and marks distances on the tape.
    b. Artist: draws organisms that were alive at each time period.
    c. Cutter: cuts out organisms drawn by artist.
    d. Attacher: attaches organisms to the time line.

2. You need to measure **65 centimeters** of white register tape from the rolls provided. This will omit the Precambrian time period. Adding 4.6 meters will allow for the inclusion of that period.

3. The measurer should begin to measure out the distances taken up by each of the time eras, periods, and epochs so that **1 million years = 1 millimeter.** (Measure from left to right—from older to more recent history.)

4. The artist should sketch at least **2 organisms from each epoch** of geologic time on the white or colored paper provided.

5. As the artist completes each sketch, the cutter should cut out the sketch and pass it on to the attacher.

6. The attacher should take each completed, cut out sketch and attach it to the time line at the appropriate time interval. This may be done by taping it or by punching a hole in the time tape and hanging the organism from the tape at the correct spot by a piece of string.

7. When complete, the tape should have each group member's name attached and should be hung with everyone else's at the designated spot inside or outside the classroom.

8. All supplies and materials must be cleaned up at your station or table in order to qualify your group for the competition that is explained below.

ON THE FOLLOWING CLASS DAY PRIZES WILL BE AWARDED. Two groups from each class and from all classes overall for the following categories: "Most Colorful" and "Most Creative"

ERA	PERIOD	EPOCH	BEGAN	LASTED	MAJOR EVENTS
			(in millions of years)		
C E N O Z O I C E R A	Quarternary	Recent	10,000 years ago to present		Civilization, humans, and modern organisms appear
		Pleistocene	2.5 m	2.5 m	"Ice Age," modern humans first appear, mammoths become extinct
	Tertiary	Pliocene	14 m	11.5 m	Birds, fish, mammals similar to modern; cooler
		Miocene	25 m	11 m	Grazing animals, modern flowering plants & trees
		Oligocene	35 m	10 m	Primitive apes, elephants, camels, & horses; milder
		Eocene	55 m	20 m	Small horses, grasslands, whales, rhinos, & monkeys
		Paleocene	70 m	15 m	Flowering plants, small mammals; different climates
M E S O Z O I C	Cretaceous		135 m	65 m	Coal swamps, fossils of trees & plants, mammals
	Jurassic		180 m	45 m	Many dinosaurs, feathered birds
	Triassic		230 m	50 m	First dinosaurs, insects, cone-bearing plants
P A L E O Z O I C E R A	Permian		285 m	55 m	First seed plants, fish, amphibians, & reptiles
	Carboniferous	Pennsylvanian	325 m	40 m	First reptiles, amphibians, & giant insects; fern trees, swamps in lowlands
		Mississippian	350 m	25 m	
	Devonian		410 m	60 m	"Age of Fish," many types of fish; first forests
	Silurian		430 m	20 m	First land plants, algae, trilobites, & coral reefs
	Ordovician		500 m	70 m	Jawless fish, great floods, algae, & trilobites
	Cambrian		600 m	100 m	Invertebrates, clams, snails, seaweed, & seas
PRECAMBRIAN		Proterozoic	4.6 billion	4 billion	Bacteria and algae appear
		Archeozoic			

Date: _____ Names:_____

HEATING/COOLING AND CRYSTALLIZATION

INTRODUCTION: When you make rock candy by hanging a string in sugar water, what determines how big the crystals will get?

OBJECTIVE: When igneous rocks are formed from molten magma, the rate of cooling determines the size of the crystals. If the rock cools over thousands of years underground (plutonic or intrusive), then it tends to have large crystals. If cooling occurs very rapidly after the molten magma has erupted through cracks in the earth's crust (volcanic or extrusive), then the rocks tend to have smaller crystals. In this lab, we will evaporate the water from a saltwater solution at different rates to observe the crystal sizes.

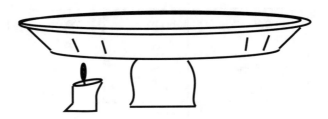

PROCEDURE:

1. Place an aluminum pan on top of a glass jar as shown in the diagram above.

2. Place the candle at one outside edge of the pan.

3. Place 12 drops of saturated salt water straight across the pan about a finger's width apart.

4. Ask your instructor to light your candle.

5. The burning candle should touch the bottom of the pan at one end of the line of drops.

6. Observe the reaction for 20 to 25 minutes.

7. At the end of the 25 minutes, feel the crystal size of each of the droplets. Record your observations on the next page.

Date: _____ Names: _____

Drop Location	Observations
Drops closest to flame	
Drops in middle of pan	
Drops farthest from flame	

QUESTIONS:

1. How does the crystal size vary? _____

_____

_____

2. How does the crystal size relate to how fast the drop evaporated? _____

_____

_____

3. Which drops are most like plutonic/intrusive rocks?_____

_____

4. Which drops are most like volcanic/extrusive rocks? _____

_____

5. What would you need to do to make big rock candy crystals?_____

_____

_____

_____

_____

Date: _____ Names: _____

GASES IN MAGMA

INTRODUCTION: When you dive into a pool, it is pretty easy to go to the bottom, but what happens when you wear a life preserver? What causes a life preserver to be able to keep you afloat?

OBJECTIVE: Molten rock inside the earth is called MAGMA. Often gases are dissolved in the magma. The gases are less dense than the surrounding material, and they rise to the surface. As they rise, other materials are carried along with them. In this activity, we will construct artificial magma and observe its reaction.

PROCEDURE: Set-up A
1. Add 2 heaping teaspoons of baking soda to your 400-mL beaker.
2. Add 300 mL water to the beaker.
3. Stir until the baking soda has dissolved.
4. Drop 2–3 mothballs into the solution.
5. Add 100 mL vinegar to the solution and stir vigorously. **This solution may bubble over!**
6. Observe.

Set-up B
1. Add 400 mL water to the beaker.
2. Add 1 Alka-Seltzer tablet to the water.
3. Drop in 2–3 kernels of popcorn or short pieces of spaghetti.
4. Observe.

OBSERVATIONS: Sketch what you see happening on the diagrams below. Use arrows to indicate direction. Also, describe your observations on the lines below.

_____   _____
_____   _____
_____   _____
_____   _____

Date: _____ Names: _____

QUESTIONS:

1. What happened to the mothballs, spaghetti, and popcorn that you dropped into the solutions?

_____

_____

_____

2. What caused this reaction to occur? _____

_____

_____

3. What were baking soda and vinegar and Alka-Seltzer providing in this activity? _____

_____

_____

4. Why are bubbles important in this reaction? _____

_____

_____

5. In this activity, what represents:

    a. the magma? _____

    b. the rocks suspended in the magma? _____

6. How is a life preserver on a human similar to bubbles surrounding a popcorn kernel in water?

_____

_____

_____

_____

Date: _____ Names: _____

PILE IT ON!

INTRODUCTION: How are the layers of the earth similar to a sandwich?

OBJECTIVE: Most of the upper layers of the earth's crust that become visible when roads are built and rivers erode have been laid down by sedimentation, one layer on top of the one below it. This process of placing the oldest layers of rock down first with younger layers on top of that is called the LAW OF SUPERPOSITION. Afterwards, different things may happen to the rock layers. If pressure causes them to buckle and form a hill, it is called an ANTICLINE. If a similar pressure causes them to buckle and form a valley, it is called a SYNCLINE. FAULTS or cracks may also occur in the layers. In this activity, we will construct such a system of rock layers using peanut butter, jelly, and bread. We will then practice identifying which layers and processes occurred in which order.

PROCEDURE: <u>CRUST CONSTRUCTION</u>

    1. Take to your table the following:
        a knife
        a paper plate
        two pieces of white bread
        one piece of wheat bread
        one blob of chunky peanut butter
        one blob of jelly

    2. Place the white bread in the middle of the paper plate. It is to be the first (and therefore, oldest) rock layer deposited.

    3. Spread a layer of chunky peanut butter on the white bread.

    4. Place the wheat bread on top of the peanut butter.

    5. Spread the jelly on top of the wheat bread.

    6. Top with another piece of white bread.

<u>CRUSTAL CHANGES</u>

7. Bend the layers upwards in the middle to create a hill (anticline).

8. Bend the layers downwards in the middle to create a valley (syncline).

9. Cut through the layers down the middle to create a fault.
    a. Lowering one side below the other creates a vertical fault.
    b. Sliding one side to the right or left of the other creates a sliding fault.

** CUT YOUR CRUST INTO AS MANY SECTIONS AS YOU HAVE PARTNERS AND EAT IT. **

Date: _____ Names: _____

QUESTIONS:

1. What does the Law of Superposition say? _____

_____

_____

2. According to that law, describe the order of the layers in your "crust."

Oldest: _____

                 _____

                 _____

                 _____

Youngest: _____

3. Sketch the anticline you constructed.

4. Sketch the syncline you constructed.

5. Place the rock layers and events sketched below in order from oldest (1) to youngest (6).

Oldest: 1. _____
             2. _____
             3. _____
             4. _____
             5. _____
Youngest: 6. _____

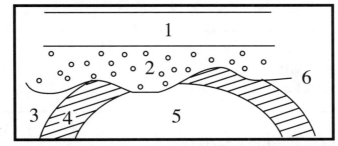

6. Place the rock layers and events sketched below in order from oldest (1) to youngest (7).

Oldest: 1. _____
             2. _____
             3. _____
             4. _____
             5. _____
             6. _____
Youngest   7. _____

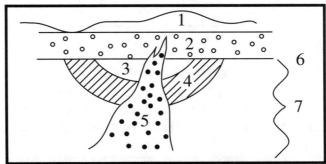

Date: _____ Names: _____

WHAT IS THE MANTLE LIKE?

INTRODUCTION: If you pull Silly Putty apart very slowly, what happens? What if you jerk a strand apart rapidly?

OBJECTIVE: In this activity, we will investigate the properties of the mantle of the earth. The mantle has the ability to behave both as a liquid (by flowing) and as a solid (by breaking and by not allowing objects to penetrate easily).

PROCEDURE:

1. Add 6 teaspoons of cornstarch to your plastic cup.

2. Add 25 mL of water to the cornstarch in the cup.

3. Use the plastic spoon to stir the solution.

4. The solution should be about as thick as pudding, soft ice cream, or yogurt.

5. Conduct each investigation described below and record your observations in the spaces provided.

INVESTIGATION	OBSERVATIONS
A. Try to stick a spoon into the "mantle."	
B. Try to stir the "mantle" rapidly.	
C. Pour into your hand. As you are pouring, have your partner "swipe" a finger through the flow.	
D. In your hands, try to roll into a ball.	

**DURING CLEANUP: a. Dump extra "mantle" into container provided.

b. Rinse cups and spoon in bucket of water provided before finishing cleanup at the sink. Cornstarch will clog drains!

40

Date: _____ Names: _____

QUESTIONS:

1. Describe two examples of how our "mantle" behaved like a liquid:

a. _____

_____

b. _____

_____

2. Describe two examples of how our "mantle" behaved like a solid:

a. _____

_____

b. _____

_____

3. How would the real mantle of the earth react under the following situations:

a. a gentle, continuous pressure. _____

_____

_____

b. a sudden, forceful impact. _____

_____

_____

4. How would you predict Silly Putty to behave under:

a. gentle pressure. _____

_____

b. sudden pressure. _____

_____

Date: _____ Names: _____

CHARACTERISTICS OF THE EARTH

INTRODUCTION: Which is a better model of the earth: a softball, a Silly Putty egg, a globe, or a hard-boiled egg?

OBJECTIVE: In order to better understand the structure of the earth, we will examine several items as models. Finally, we will examine one of the best models in order to see a comparison of the size of the layers of the earth.

crust ———— lithosphere (brittle layer)
mantle
outer core   asthenosphere (fluid layer)
inner core

PROCEDURE: I. ANY OLD MODEL
    1. For each item listed below, list at least 3 reasons why it would be a good model of the earth, as well as 3 reasons why it would not be a good model of the earth.

A. Softball
Good:

_____

_____

_____

Bad:

_____

_____

_____

B. Silly Putty Container
Good:

_____

_____

_____

Bad:

_____

_____

_____

C. Globe
Good:

_____

_____

_____

Bad:

_____

_____

_____

QUESTIONS:

1. What characteristics seemed to make objects good models of the earth? _____

_____

2. What characteristics seemed to make objects bad models of the earth? _____

_____

3. Of the three models, which seemed like the best model? Why? _____

_____

Date: _____ Names: _____

PROCEDURE: II. AN EGG-CELLENT MODEL

          1. Using the egg as a model of the earth, evaluate it by listing characteristics that make it a good model, as well as characteristics that make it a bad model.

Good: Bad:

_____   _____

_____   _____

_____   _____

_____   _____

          2. "Plates" can be placed on the egg by **gently** dropping it on the table to crack the shell. Then use the marker to trace the outline of the major cracks.

          3. The inside of the egg can be seen and compared to the structure of the earth if the egg is cut open on its long side.

          4. Sketch the layers of the egg in the space below.

QUESTIONS:

1. How do the layers of the egg compare to the layers of the earth?

      a. _____

      b. _____

      c. _____

      d. _____

2. Describe two other ways that the egg compares to the earth.

      a. _____

_____

      b. _____

_____

Date: _____   Names: _____

CONVECTION AND MAGMA

INTRODUCTION: If you fill a soft-drink bottle with hot, colored water and set it in the bottom of a bucket filled with cold water, what will happen to the colored liquid?

OBJECTIVE: The fluid property of the mantle allows the crustal plates to move on the surface of the earth, but it also allows other activities to occur within it. Material gets moved around by a process called CONVECTION. Warm material (or less dense material) moves upwards while cooler (more dense) material moves downwards creating currents of flowing material within the mantle. In this activity, we will observe the effects of temperature differences on convection.

PROCEDURE: I. <u>HOT STUFF RISES</u>

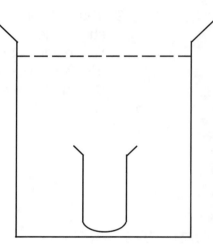

1. Place 2 drops of food coloring in the small bottle.
2. Fill this bottle with hot water.
3. Fill the 400-mL beaker to the 350-mL mark with tap water.
4. Gently lower the small bottle into the beaker of tap water.
5. Observe the reaction and sketch what you see on the diagram at right.
** If you're not convinced that this has something to do with temperature differences, try it again with cool water in the small bottle.

II. <u>CONVECTION CURRENTS</u>

1. Place the clear plastic pan on a tripod of upside-down cups.
2. Fill this plastic pan 3/4 full of tap water.
3. For each set of conditions described below, gently place a drop of food coloring into the pan with the dropper as described. Then, sketch a side view of what happens. (Observe for 2 to 3 minutes each time.)

a. Place a drop on center bottom of the pan.

b. Place a cup of hot water under the center of the pan. Place a drop on the center bottom of the pan.

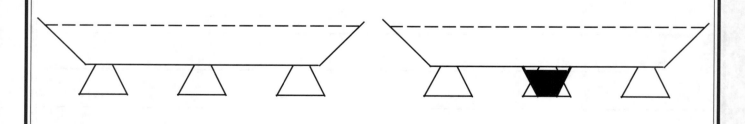

Date: _____ Names: _____

c. With the cup of hot water underneath, place a drop at the side on the bottom of the pan.

d. With the cup of hot water underneath, place a drop at the side on the surface of the water.

QUESTIONS:

1. What happened to the colored, hot water in the little bottle when you placed it in the cold water?

_____

_____

2. What caused this reaction?_____

_____

_____

3. What happened in each reaction below:

a. drop was placed on center bottom, no heat? _____

_____

b. drop was placed on center bottom, with heat?_____

_____

c. drop was placed on side bottom, with heat?_____

_____

d. drop was placed on side top, with heat? _____

_____

4. Where does the colored drop rise? _____

sink? _____

Date: _____ Names: _____

VOLCANO TYPE AND LOCATION

INTRODUCTION: Why are some rocks in your yard white while some are black and white and others are blue? If rocks come from beneath the surface of the earth, do different volcanoes produce different lava?

OBJECTIVE: The location of a volcano tends to determine the composition of the volcanic rock resulting from the volcano. The major material present in volcanic rock is SILICA. Volcanic rock considered high in silica content (more than 66%) usually appears grey or pink and is called RHYOLITE. This type of material is usually found at convergent boundaries where some crustal material is subducted and rises to the surface. Rock that is considered to have a medium silica content (52%–66%) usually appears dark grey and is called ANDESITE. This material usually appears at subduction zones as well—without rising up toward the surface. The third type of material is low in silica content (less than 52%), appears black, and is called BASALT. This material generally is found at divergent plate boundaries or at HOT SPOTS (areas under the crust where there is a lot of activity, like the Hawaiian Islands). In this activity, we will plot the locations of the different types of volcanoes and note their relation to types of plate boundaries.

PROCEDURE:
      1. On the attached data sheet, identify each volcano as rhyolite, andesite, or basalt.
      2. On the map provided, plot the different volcanoes listed on page 47.
      3. Plot the volcano at the correct longitude and latitude.
      4. Use the following key to code the volcanoes:
            + = rhyolite
            • = andesite
            ♦ = basalt

QUESTIONS:
1. Along what outline do the volcanoes fall? _____

_____

2. Are all volcanoes located along this outline? Where are the others? _____

_____

3. What is an area, such as that where the stray volcanoes are located, called? _____

4. Which type of volcanic material appears: a. black? _____
   b. dark grey? _____   c. grey, pink? _____

5. At what type of plate boundaries do the following volcanic materials appear:
   a. rhyolite?_____   b. andesite? _____
   c. basalt? _____

Date: _____ Names: _____

Volcano Location	Latitude	Longitude	% Composition			Rock Type
			silica	aluminum	iron	
1. Lassen, CA	40 N	121 W	57.3	18.3	6.2	_____
2. Crater Lake, OR	43 N	122 W	55.1	18.0	7.1	_____
3. Mt. Rainier, WA	47 N	122 W	62.2	17.1	5.1	_____
4. Mt. Baker, WA	49 N	122 W	57.4	16.6	8.1	_____
5. Yellowstone, WY	45 N	111 W	75.5	13.3	1.9	_____
6. Craters of the Moon, ID	43 N	114 W	53.5	14.0	15.2	_____
7. San Francisco Peaks, AZ	35 N	112 W	61.2	17.0	5.7	_____
8. Paricutín, Mexico	19 N	102 W	55.1	19.0	7.3	_____
9. Popocatépetl, Mexico	19 N	98 W	62.5	16.6	4.9	_____
10. Mt. Pelée, Martinique	15 N	61 W	65.0	17.8	4.5	_____
11. Santa María, Guatemala	15 N	92 W	59.4	19.9	5.9	_____
12. Mt. Misery, St. Kitts	17 N	63 W	59.8	18.3	7.3	_____
13. Cotopaxi, Equador	1 S	78 W	56.2	15.3	9.7	_____
14. El Misti, Peru	16 S	71 W	60.1	19.0	5.0	_____
15. Katmai, AK	58 N	155 W	76.9	12.2	1.4	_____
16. Adak, Aleutians	52 N	177 W	60.0	17.0	6.9	_____
17. Umnak Islands, Aleutians	53 N	169 W	52.5	15.1	12.8	_____
18. Kamchatka, Russia	57 N	160 E	60.6	16.4	7.9	_____
19. Fuji, Honshu, Japan	35 N	139 E	49.8	20.6	11.2	_____
20. Izu-Hakone, Honshu, Japan	35 N	139 E	53.8	14.8	13.0	_____
21. Mayon, Philippines	13 N	124 E	53.1	20.0	8.2	_____
22. Krakatau, Indonesia	6 S	105 E	67.3	15.6	4.3	_____
23. Karkar, New Guinea	5 S	146 E	60.1	16.4	9.6	_____
24. Mauna Loa, HI	19 N	156 W	49.6	13.2	11.9	_____
25. Galápagos Islands	1 S	91 W	48.4	15.4	11.8	_____
26. Mariana Islands	16 N	145 E	51.2	17.3	10.9	_____
27. Auckland, New Zealand	38 S	176 E	49.3	15.6	11.9	_____
28. Tahiti	18 S	149 W	44.3	14.3	12.4	_____
29. Samoa	13 S	172 W	48.4	13.3	12.3	_____
30. Surtsey, Iceland	63 N	20 W	50.8	13.6	12.5	_____
31. Mid-ocean Ridge	60 N	18 W	48.2	16.5	11.7	_____
32. Kilimanjaro, Tanzania	3 S	37 E	45.6	10.3	12.6	_____

Date: _____ Names: _____

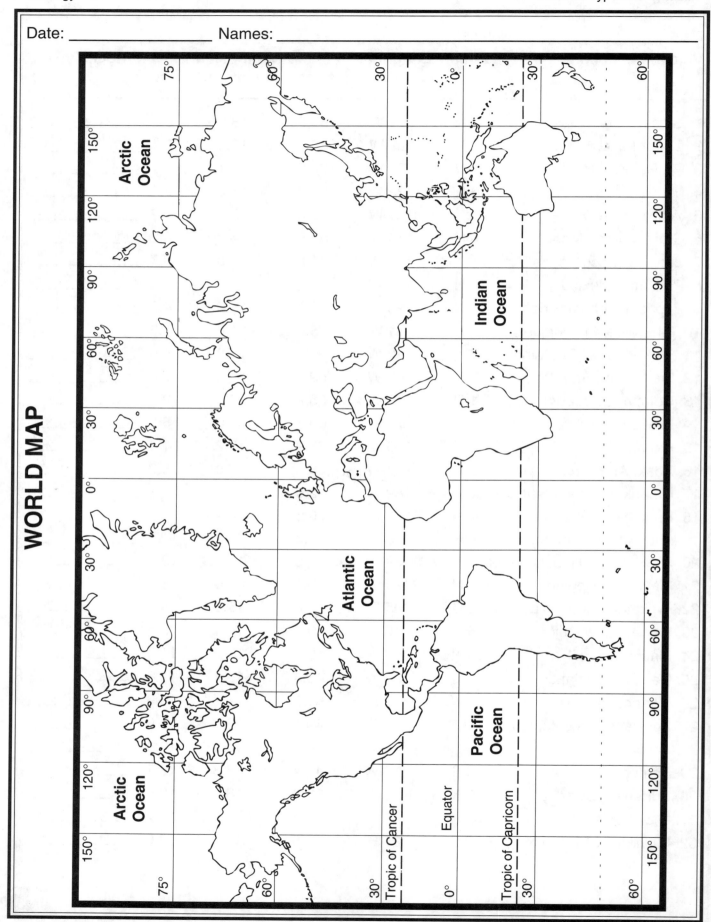

WORLD MAP

Arctic Ocean

Arctic Ocean

Atlantic Ocean

Pacific Ocean

Indian Ocean

75°
150°
120°
90°
60°
30°
0°
30°
60°
90°
120°
150°
75°
60°

Tropic of Cancer
Equator
Tropic of Capricorn

Date: _____ Names: _____

LOCATING EARTHQUAKE EPICENTERS

INTRODUCTION: Early settlers were able to tell when horses or trains were coming by putting an ear to the ground to listen for the sound waves. Earthquake shock waves can be detected in a similar, but more sophisticated, way.

OBJECTIVE: When an earthquake occurs, shock waves are sent out in all directions. There are two main types of shock waves. Waves that travel rapidly and arrive quickly at places away from the earthquake are called PRIMARY waves (P-waves). Waves that travel more slowly, but do more damage, are called SECONDARY waves (S-waves). S-waves arrive after P-waves at places away from the earthquake.

The place where rocks shift and cause earthquakes inside the earth is called the FOCUS. The point on the surface of the earth just above the focus is called the EPICENTER. In this activity, we will use P- and S-wave data to calculate where earthquake epicenters occur.

PROCEDURE: <u>EXAMPLE</u>

1. The difference in arrival times of P- and S-waves for our example earthquake are listed in the chart on page 50.
2. The P- and S-wave differences are related to the distance of the city from the earthquake epicenter.
3. Find the time difference on the center column of the chart (minutes and seconds).
4. Find that time on the vertical axis of the graph, and follow that mark over to the right to the curved line on the graph.
5. From the curved line on the graph, go straight down to the "Distance to the Epicenter" (kilometers) at the bottom.
6. Record this distance in the example chart for "Distance to Epicenter."
7. Repeat this process for the other two cities.
8. On the map of the United States, open your compass to the distance for city #1. Use the scale key on the map to set your compass accurately.
9. Put the compass point on that city (#1), and draw a circle of the correct radius around the city.
10. Repeat steps 8 and 9 for the other two cities.
11. The point where **all three circles cross** represents the epicenter of the earthquake.
12. Record the epicenter location in the space below the map.

<u>TRIALS 1 AND 2</u>

1. Repeat steps 1–12 for the two sets of earthquake data on pages 51 and 52.

QUESTIONS:

1. Which earthquake waves arrive at places away from the earthquake first? _____

Second? _____

Date: _____ Names: _____

2. What is the area on the surface of the earth directly above the focus of an earthquake called?

_____

3. How are P- and S-wave arrival time differences related to the distance of a city away from an

epicenter? _____

_____

_____

4. Why is it necessary to find the distance from the epicenter for three cities in order to pinpoint the

epicenter of an earthquake? _____

_____

_____

_____

EXAMPLE

City	Difference in P- and S-Wave Arrival Time	Distance (km)
Denver	2 minutes, 25 seconds	
Miami	5 minutes, 40 seconds	
Houston	4 minutes, 10 seconds	

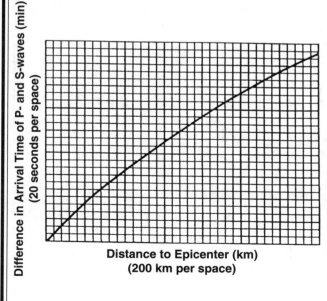

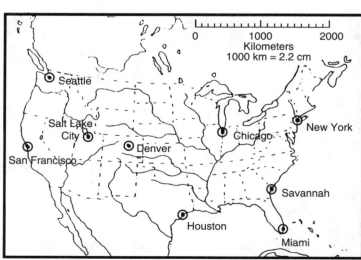

EPICENTER: _____

Date: _____ Names: _____

TRIAL #1

City	Difference in P- and S-Wave Arrival Time	Distance (km)
Chicago	2 minutes, 30 seconds	
Salt Lake City	3 minutes, 00 seconds	
New York	3 minutes, 40 seconds	

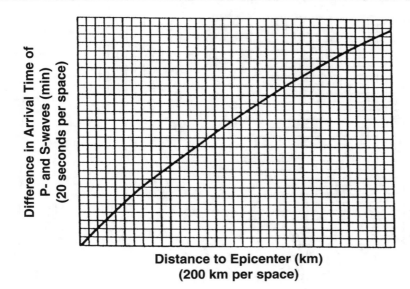

Distance to Epicenter (km)
(200 km per space)

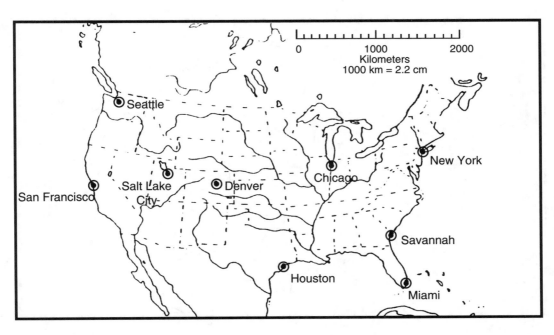

EPICENTER: _____

51

Date: _____   Names: _____

TRIAL #2

City	Difference in P- and S-Wave Arrival Time	Distance (km)
Savannah	5 minutes, 30 seconds	
Miami	5 minutes, 50 seconds	
Seattle	2 minutes, 00 seconds	

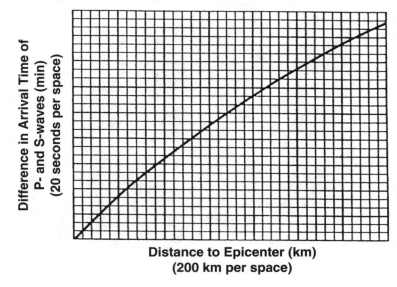

Distance to Epicenter (km)
(200 km per space)

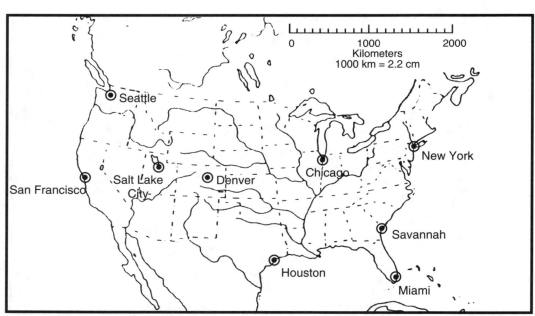

EPICENTER: _____

Date: _____ Names: _____

IDENTIFYING ROCKS AND MINERALS

INTRODUCTION: If you found two rocks in your yard that looked almost alike, but a geologist told you that they were two different types of rock, how could you figure out which one was which?

OBJECTIVE: Rocks are made up of several different minerals. Rocks can be identified by the minerals in them, while minerals can be identified by characteristic properties. These properties include: (1) color, (2) size of crystals, (3) cleavage (breaking plane), (4) streak color, and (5) hardness. In this activity, we will examine some of the characteristics of common minerals and rocks in order to name them.

PROCEDURE:
   1. At each lab station there is a rock/mineral sample.
   2. You will be allowed three minutes at each lab station to:
       a. describe the color of the rock/mineral.
       b. describe the grain size of the rock/mineral.
       c. conduct a streak test (by scraping rock across the unglazed side of a ceramic tile) and recording the color of the streak for the rock/mineral.
       d. describe the cleavage (broken at 90-degree angles, appears to be layered, angles irregular) of the rock/mineral.
       e. conduct a hardness test (by scraping rock on items to see if it scratches them—see scale below) of the rock/mineral.

   Moh's Scale of Hardness
   1.0–2.5   Won't scratch a fingernail.
   2.5–3.5   Scratches fingernail, but won't scratch a penny.
   3.5–5.5   Scratches penny, but won't scratch glass.
   5.5–6.5   Scratches glass, but won't scratch steel.
   6.5–10   Scratches steel.

   3. Record each observation in the chart on page 54.
   4. At the end of the activity, use the key on page 55 to identify the rocks/minerals based on your observations. Write in the rock/mineral name in the row next to the appropriate set of observations in the chart.
   5. Finally, answer the following questions based on your observations.

QUESTIONS:
1. What are five characteristics that can be used to identify rocks/minerals? a. _____
   b. _____   c. _____   d. _____   e. _____
2. What is the difference between rocks and minerals? _____
_____
3. What is the range of hardness on the Moh's scale? _____
_____

Date: _____ Names: _____

ROCK TYPE: _____

LAB STATION	COLOR	STREAK COLOR	CLEAVAGE	HARDNESS	ROCK/MINERAL
1					
2					
3					
4					
5					
6					
7					
8					
9					
10					

Date: _____   Names: _____

ROCK AND MINERAL KEY

| Grain Size | Streak Color | Cleavage | Hardness | Rock/Mineral Name |

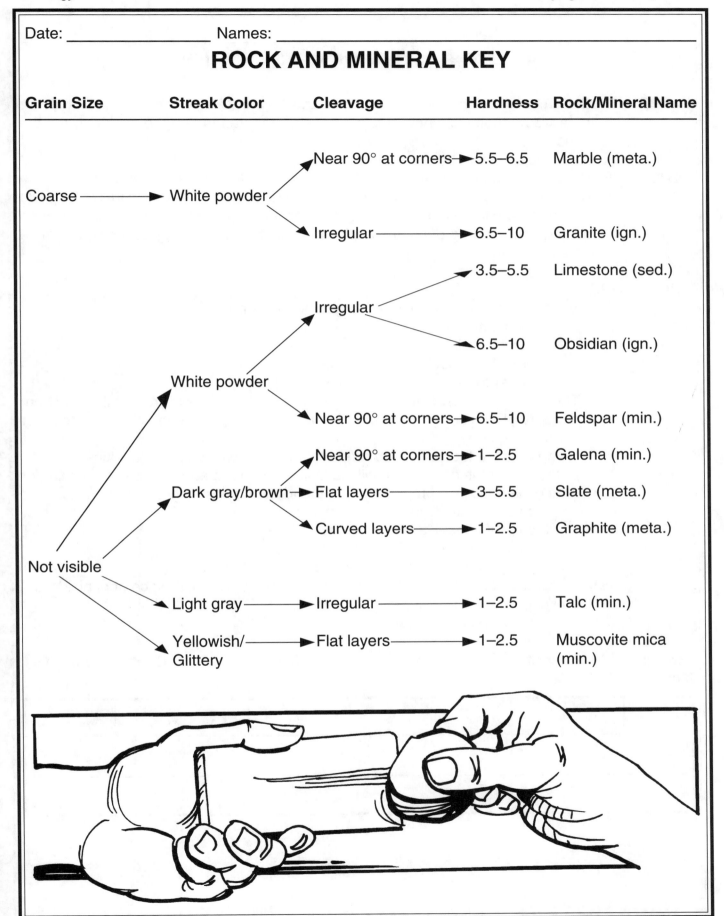

Coarse ⟶ White powder
- Near 90° at corners ➤ 5.5–6.5 → Marble (meta.)
- Irregular ➤ 6.5–10 → Granite (ign.)

Not visible ⟶ White powder
- Irregular
  - 3.5–5.5 → Limestone (sed.)
  - 6.5–10 → Obsidian (ign.)
- Near 90° at corners ➤ 6.5–10 → Feldspar (min.)

Not visible ⟶ Dark gray/brown
- Near 90° at corners ➤ 1–2.5 → Galena (min.)
- Flat layers ➤ 3–5.5 → Slate (meta.)
- Curved layers ➤ 1–2.5 → Graphite (meta.)

Not visible ⟶ Light gray ➤ Irregular ➤ 1–2.5 → Talc (min.)

Not visible ⟶ Yellowish/Glittery ➤ Flat layers ➤ 1–2.5 → Muscovite mica (min.)

Date: _____ Names: _____

IF THE EARTH WERE A COOKIE

INTRODUCTION: If chocolate chips were fossil fuels and the only thing you could use to mine for them was a toothpick, how would you keep from tearing up the cookie to get the chips?

OBJECTIVE: The energy that produces the electricity that we take for granted often comes from the movement of water or from the burning of fossil fuels like coal. In this activity, we will investigate the effects of mining for a resource such as coal. Since coal is often located deep underground, the mining of coal often causes a great deal of harm to the ecosystem.

PROCEDURE:

1. Each group member will need to get the following supplies:
   1 toothpick
   1 soft chocolate chip cookie
   1 crunchy chocolate chip cookie
   1 paper towel
2. The cookie represents the earth, and the chocolate chips represent the coal from the earth. Each chocolate chip is enough "coal" to provide the electricity for your town for one day.
3. Using only the toothpick, you are to "mine" for the chips in the cookies.
4. At the end of the activity you will have to "pay" for damage done to the earth (for land reclamation and restoration) in the form of chips at the following rate:
   1 chip if cookie is intact with only pits
   2 chips if cookie is in 2–3 pieces
   3 chips if cookie is in 4–8 pieces
   4 chips if cookie is in crumbs (more than 8 pieces)
5. If your tool (toothpick) breaks and needs to be replaced, replacement picks cost one chip.
6. Record your results below:

Group Member	Number of Chips Mined	Effects on Cookie (Earth)	Cost	Total Gain
1				
2				
3				

Date: _____   Names: _____

QUESTIONS:

1. How many days of energy did your group gain? _____
_____

2. Which land type (cookie type) was easiest to mine? Why? _____
_____

_____

3. What land type is similar to:

     a. the soft cookie? _____

     b. the crunchy cookie? _____

4. What type of mining technique worked best? _____
_____

5. How is land reclaimed after mining? _____
_____

_____

_____

GEOLOGY ANSWER KEYS

HEATING/COOLING AND CRYSTALLIZATION (page 35)
1. Crystals near the flame are powdery while those farther away are grainy.
2. The faster the drop evaporated, the more powdery and the smaller the crystal size.
3. Drops that evaporate very slowly (farther from the flame) are most like the rocks that cool slowly with the earth and have larger crystals.
4. Drops that evaporate quickly (closer to the flame) are most like the rocks that cool quickly on the surface of the earth and have smaller crystals.
5. Larger rock candy crystals can be made by allowing the crystallization to occur over a longer period of time.

GASES IN MAGMA (page 37)
1. The spaghetti, mothballs, and popcorn become covered in bubbles and rise to the top of the liquid, release the bubbles, and then fall back to the bottom.
2. The bubbles that attach cause the objects to become less dense than water so they rise. When the bubbles are released, the object is once again more dense than water and falls back to the bottom.
3. Baking soda and vinegar and Alka-Seltzer produce the gas bubbles in the liquid.
4. The bubbles are necessary to change the density of the objects so they will move.
5a. the liquids; b. the objects
6. The life preserver is actually like a giant air bubble that decreases the density of humans to less than that of water so they will float.

PILE IT ON! (page 39)
1. Older layers of rock are deposited, then younger layers of rock are laid down on top of them.
2. Oldest: white bread
             chunky peanut butter
             wheat bread
             jelly
Youngest: white bread

3. 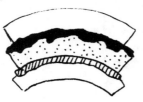   4.

5. Oldest to Youngest: 5, 4, 3, 6, 2, 1
6. Oldest to Youngest: 4, 3, 7, 6, 2, 1, 5
Layers 4 and 3 were deposited. Layer 7 folded, creating a syncline whose top was eroded (6).
Layers 2 and 1 were deposited, and the intrusion (5) jutted through.

WHAT IS THE MANTLE LIKE? (page 41)

1. Answers will vary: a. The solution could be poured;
   b. The solution turns into a puddle when you stop rolling it.
2. Answers will vary: a. The spoon will not go into the solution rapidly, it bounces out;
   b. The solution can be rolled into a ball if you roll it continuously.
3a. The mantle would flow; b. The mantle would crack and shift.
4a. The Silly Putty would stretch and bend;
   b. The Silly Putty would break off or shatter (if struck by a hammer).

CHARACTERISTICS OF THE EARTH (pages 42–43)

** All observations are acceptable.

I. 1. Answers will vary, but should include: Layers, approximate shape, marking on the surface, and so on.
2. Answers will vary, but should include: Not exact same shape, size, make-up, proportion of layers to one another, and so on.
3. Answers will vary.
II. 1a. The shell is like the earth's crust.
   b. The white is like the earth's mantle.
   c. The yellow is like the earth's outer core.
   d. A dot in the center of the yellow is like the earth's inner core.
2. Answers will vary: The shape of the earth is kind of egg-shaped. When you crack the eggshell, the cracks are similar to the earth's plate boundaries.

CONVECTION AND MAGMA (page 45)

1. The colored water rose up out of the little bottle.
2. Hot water is less dense than cold water.
3a. If the water is still, with no heat, everything just sits there.
   b. With heat, the colored drop will rise to the top, move to the side, and fall.
   c. The colored drop will cross the bottom toward the heat source then rise to the top.
   d. The colored drop will fall to the bottom, move toward the heat source, then rise to the top.
4. The colored drop rises over the heat source and falls when it is away from the heat.

VOLCANO TYPE AND LOCATION (page 46)

1. Volcanoes are generally located along plate boundaries.
2. No. Some volcanoes are located in "hot spots" in the middle of plates.
3. Hot spots.
4a. basalt; b. andesite; c. rhyolite
5a. convergent; b. subduction zones; c. divergent

VOLCANO ROCK TYPE (page 47)

1. andesite	2. andesite	3. andesite
4. andesite	5. rhyolite	6. andesite
7. andesite	8. andesite	9. andesite
10. andesite	11. andesite	12. andesite
13. andesite	14. andesite	15. rhyolite
16. andesite	17. andesite	18. andesite
19. basalt	20. andesite	21. andesite
22. rhyolite	23. andesite	24. basalt
25. basalt	26. basalt	27. basalt
28. basalt	29. basalt	30. basalt
31. basalt	32. basalt	

LOCATING EARTHQUAKE EPICENTERS (page 49–52)

1. Primary; secondary
2. Epicenter
3. The greater the difference between arrival times of P- and S-waves, the farther the city is from the earthquake epicenter.
4. One city provides a radius on which the epicenter occurs. Two cities narrow the location to the two points of intersection between the two cities. The third circle will intersect at one of the two points of intersection.
Example: Denver d = 1,400 km, Miami d = 400 km, Houston d = 2,700 km; Epicenter = Seattle.
Trial #1: Chicago d = 1,500 km, Salt Lake City d = 1,800 km, New York d = 2,300 km; Epicenter = Houston.
Trial #2: Savannah d = 3,800 km, Miami d = 4,200 km, Seattle d = 1,200 km; Epicenter = San Francisco.

IDENTIFYING ROCKS AND MINERALS (page 53)

1a. color; b. crystal size; c. cleavage; d. streak color; e. hardness
2. Rocks are made up of several different minerals.
3.
      1.0–2.5   Won't scratch a fingernail
      2.5–3.5   Scratches fingernail, not a penny
      3.5–5.5   Scratches penny, not glass
      5.5–6.5   Scratches glass, not steel
      6.5–10   Scratches steel

IF THE EARTH WERE A COOKIE (page 57)

1. Answer depends on group data.
2. The soft cookie was easier to mine because it was easier to dig into.
3a. Sandstone (or other softer rock types)
  b. Quartz, granite (or other harder rock types)
4. Answers will vary according to student techniques.
5. Answers will vary, but might include: Land is filled in and grass is sown, or water is allowed to fill quarries for recreation or wildlife use.

OCEANOGRAPHY INDEX AND MATERIALS LIST

WATER: THE MICKEY MOUSE MOLECULE 63
Patterns (see page 64), scissors, and glue.

WATER ACTIVITIES 65
Five lab station set-ups:
a. two pennies, water, soapy water, two droppers
b. bubble solution of water, glycerine, and detergent; clean straws; and meterstick.
c. pan of water, aluminum foil
d. lots of clay balls, toothpicks, soap solution from "b"
e. meterstick, water dropper, plastic wrap

SURFACE TENSION 67
A penny, nickel, dime, quarter, water, and dropper are needed for part 1. For part 2, the five
containers listed in the chart on page 67 (or five others) and lots of pennies are needed.

ROCK BOTTOM 69
Sink or bucket filled with dark water (colored to conceal the bottom) with bricks on bottom,
string, fishing weight, metric ruler, and grid or meterstick to go across "ocean." The grid can
be made by cutting wire mesh into strips that are about 5 inches wide and long enough to
reach from one side to the other of the sinks, buckets, or rectangle trash cans. Grid size
should be 1 cm to 1 inch.

DENSITY OF SOLUTIONS 71
Thick raw potato slices, clear straws cut in half, four droppers, and four solutions of different
colors (alcohol, water, salt water, glycerine).

SALINITY OF SOLUTIONS 73
Same as in Density of Solutions except solutions are saturated salt water, 50% and 25%
saturated salt water, and tap water.

SALTY SITUATIONS 75
250-mL beaker, beaker tongs, ice cubes, salt, heat source, thermometers, teaspoons.

SALINITY TESTING 77
Three 4-inch straws, clay, 250-mL beaker, gunshot pellets, ruler, water, saturated salt
water, and 50% and 25% saturated salt water.

DAVEY JONES'S LOCKER 80
Three small vials with corks; gunshot pellets; tall graduated cylinders; blue, cold, salty water;
and warm, yellow, fresh water.

HEAT CAPACITY OF SAND AND WATER 82
Two cups, heat lamp or sunny day outside, thermometers, sand, and water.

SURFACE CURRENTS **84**
     AQ–1000 from NOVOSTAR DESIGNS (some shampoos with a "pearly" appearance will
     undergo the same reactions), large pan, large chunk of clay, drinking straw, maps of coastal
     outlines from pages 85–86 enlarged and laminated, and wax pencil.

WATER CYCLE TALES **88**
     Activity sheet provided.

ANSWER KEYS **89**

Date: _____ Names: _____

WATER: THE MICKEY MOUSE MOLECULE

INTRODUCTION: Water droplets are round, but if you kept dividing one into smaller and smaller pieces, what would an individual molecule look like?

OBJECTIVE: Water, like all matter, is made of tiny particles called atoms. Atoms are made up of protons, which have a positive charge, electrons, which have a negative charge, and neutrons, which have no charge. Protons and neutrons are located in the center, or nucleus, of the atom while electrons spin around the outside of the nucleus. Electrons are organized in "energy levels." The closest level to the nucleus is only able to hold two electrons; the next level can hold eight. When a bond forms between two hydrogens and one oxygen to form a water molecule, a "sharing" of electrons occurs between the hydrogens and the oxygen. This sharing fills the first (and only) energy level in each of the hydrogen atoms, as well as the second energy level in the oxygen atom.

Hydrogen end is positive

Oxygen end is negative

Because both hydrogens are located nearer to one end of the oxygen and their protons are nearest that end of the molecule, that end tends to be positively charged. The other end is negatively charged. This causes the water molecule to be called a POLAR MOLECULE and results in the strong attractive forces between water molecules because opposite charges attract.

PROCEDURE:
1. From page 64, cut out all of the atoms, protons, neutrons, and electrons.
2. Assemble the water molecule from the cut out pieces so that it resembles the diagram above.
3. When your molecule is complete, attach it to your classmates' completed molecules to form a larger water droplet. Remember, opposite sides attract.

QUESTIONS:

1. Where are the following located?   Protons: _____

Neutrons: _____ Electrons: _____

2. How many electrons can fit in the first energy level? _____ Second energy level? _____

3. How do the hydrogens and oxygen fill their energy levels? _____

_____

_____

4. Why is water called a "polar molecule"? _____

_____

5. What is the basic shape of water molecules? _____

_____

63

Date: _____ Names: _____

+ 8 Protons

8 Neutrons

OXYGEN NUCLEUS

e _ e _ e _ e _

e _ e _ e _ e _

OXYGEN ELECTRONS

OXYGEN

HYDROGEN

HYDROGEN

e _   e _

HYDROGEN ELECTRONS

1 Proton +

1 Proton +

HYDROGEN NUCLEI

Date: _____   Names: _____

WATER ACTIVITIES

INTRODUCTION: How will a drop of water act if you try to stretch it? How many drops of water can you pile on a penny? What is the biggest bubble you can make with soapy water?

OBJECTIVE: In this series of activities, we will investigate some of the unique properties of water.

PROCEDURE:
1. We will visit 5 different lab stations while doing this activity.
2. Make sure that your observations are written in for the correct activity, because you may do the activities in a different order than listed here.

<u>PILE IT ON</u>
1. Make sure the two pennies at this station are dry.
2. Estimate the number of drops of water or soapy water that can be piled on the penny before it spills over.

     ESTIMATE: Water _____   Soapy Water _____
     ACTUAL AMOUNT: Water _____   Soapy Water _____

3. Gently place drops of water/soapy water on the pennies until the water spills over. Don't forget to count the number of drops and record them above.
4. Create a graph showing your data by shading in the correct number of drops on the "dropper" graph below.

WATER

SOAPY

46 44 42 40 38 36 34 32 30 28 26 24 22 20 18 16 14 12 10 8 6 4 2
NUMBER OF DROPS OF WATER/SOAPY WATER

<u>BUBBLE TROUBLE</u>
1. Pour a puddle of bubble solution on the counter or in the pan provided.
2. Place your straw in the solution, trapping some of the solution in the straw.
3. Gently blow into the straw in order to create as large a bubble as possible.
4. Just before (or just after, if working on a countertop) the bubble pops, measure its diameter using metric units.
5. Record your diameter.

     DIAMETER: _____ cm _____ cm _____ cm _____ cm
                trial 1   trial 2   trial 3   average

Date: _____ Names: _____

FOLD AND FLOAT

1. Estimate the number of times that you can fold a 10 cm X 10 cm piece of aluminum foil in half before it sinks.
2. Record your estimate below.
    ESTIMATED NUMBER OF FOLDS: _____

3. Fold the foil once across its midpoint (in half) making sure to press all air out from between the layers.
4. Place the folded foil in the pan of water to see if it will float.
5. Repeat steps 3 and 4 until the foil sinks.
6. Record the maximum number of folds in the floating foil below.
    NUMBER OF FOLDS: _____

WINDOW PANES

1. Use the clay balls and toothpicks provided to construct each shape in the chart below.
2. Hold the shape by a clay ball and dip it into the soapy water solution.
3. Remove the shape and count the number of windowpanes created by the soapy water between the toothpicks.
4. **Don't just guess! The number will surprise you!**
5. Record the number of flat windowpanes in the space underneath each shape in the chart.

SHAPES						
NUMBER OF FLAT SURFACES						

STRETCHING AND DRAGGING WATER

A. STRETCHING WATER

1. Place 1 dropper full of water on the plastic beside the meterstick.
2. Using 2 toothpicks, spread the water droplet as long as possible.
3. Record the length of the water droplet below.

LENGTH: _____ cm _____ cm _____ cm _____ cm
           trial 1   trial 2   trial 3   average

B. DRAGGING WATER

1. Place 1 dropper full of water on the plastic beside the meterstick.
2. Start the timer, and with the toothpick, drag the entire water droplet the length of the plastic as quickly as possible. **No tiny droplets may be left behind!**
3. Record your time in the space below.

TIME: _____ sec. _____ sec. _____ sec. _____ sec.
         trial 1   trial 2   trial 3   average

Date: _____ Names: _____

SURFACE TENSION

INTRODUCTION: How can some insects walk on water? Why don't their skinny little feet go right through the surface of the water, causing them to sink?

OBJECTIVE: Liquids, especially water, are subjected to a unique force called SURFACE TENSION that minimizes surface area. Surface tension results from the strong force of attraction between water molecules. Surface water molecules are attracted more to one another than to other objects, therefore water can be "piled up" above the top of a container and more dense objects (like insects) can float (or walk) on water.

PROCEDURE: I. <u>A Pile of Water</u>
    1. On each of the 4 coins provided, place drops of water, counting each drop as you add it until the water spills over the edge of the coin.
    2. Record the number of drops that each coin held in the chart below.

COIN	NUMBER OF DROPS OF WATER
Penny	
Nickel	
Dime	
Quarter	

II. <u>How Many Is Too Many?</u>
1. Choose one of the containers provided.
2. Place the container in the pan.
3. Fill the container so that the water inside is level with the top of the container.
4. Drop pennies into the container until the water spills over the top, counting the pennies as you add them.
5. Record the number of pennies you added in the chart below.
6. Repeat this procedure for the other containers.

CONTAINER	NUMBER OF PENNIES ADDED
Flask	
Graduated Cylinder	
Beaker	
Plastic Cup	
Petri Dish	

Date: _____ Names: _____

QUESTIONS:

1. Which coin held more water drops? Why? _____

_____

_____

_____

2. Which container held the most pennies? _____

_____

3. What relationship is there between the size of the opening of the container and the number of pennies that can be added to the container?

_____

_____

_____

4. Describe four examples of surface tension at work.

    a. _____

_____

    b. _____

_____

    c. _____

_____

    d. _____

_____

Date: _____ Names: _____

ROCK BOTTOM

INTRODUCTION: In the park lake there is supposed to be a deep area where lots of fish live. How could you find that deep area?

OBJECTIVE: Ocean floor topography is studied and mapped by using sound waves that are bounced off the floor of the ocean. The time it takes the waves to reach the floor and return to the surface is determined by the depth to which the waves must travel before they strike the bottom and return. Originally, such investigations were done by dropping a weight to the ocean floor and measuring its depth by the line tied to it. For this reason, it is only recently, with the invention of the SONAR equipment described above, that the deepest areas of the ocean have been mapped.

PROCEDURE:
1. In the sink or bucket at your lab station a miniature "ocean" has been constructed.
2. The ocean floor is not flat.
3. We will investigate the topography of the ocean floor by using the old "sounding" method of dropping a weight into the ocean and measuring the depth on its line.
   a. Across the top of each ocean is a wire grid. Numbers are marked on the grid so that you can describe your location.
   b. From your boat on the surface of your ocean, you will drop a weight on a string, measure its depth in negative centimeters (since the distance is beneath the surface), and record that depth in the chart provided.
4. There is a catch! During the first part of the investigation, you only get to make 5 drops in order to predict the entire shape of our ocean floor. (This is because it costs lots of money to make each drop.)
5. Choose the 5 points for the first test, make the drops, record the data in the chart, and then graph your results using a dotted line (- - - -) on the graph provided.
6. **After the 5 test points have been graphed,** you will receive unlimited funds to drop at every point that you didn't already test.
7. You will then drop the weight at all the remaining points, measure the depth on the string, record the depths in the chart, and graph those points using a solid line (——) to connect the dots.

Test Points	Depth		Points	Depth		Points	Depth		Points	Depth

Date: _____ Names: _____

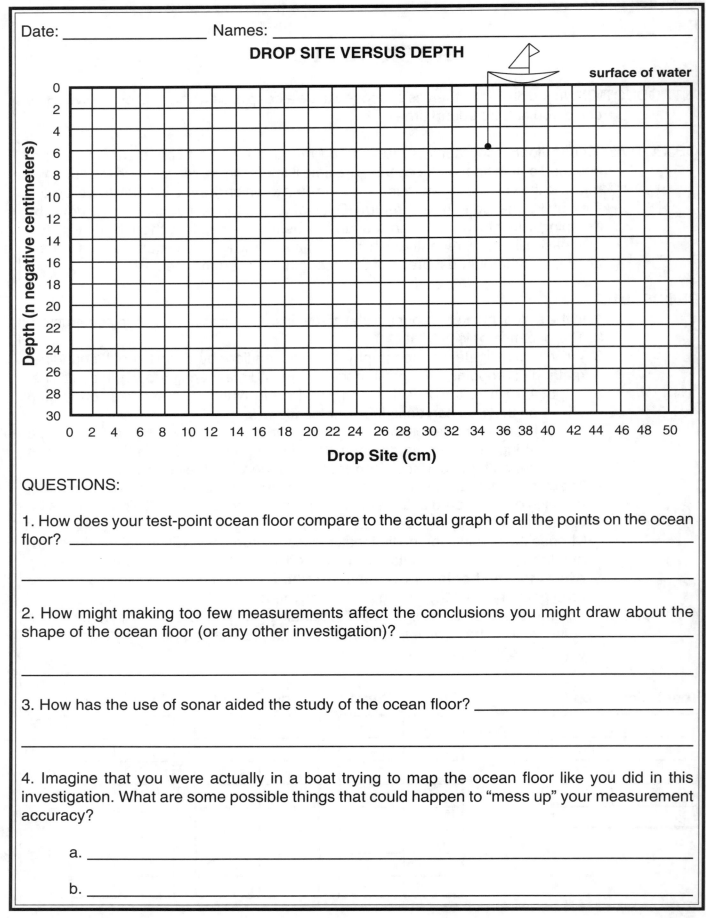

DROP SITE VERSUS DEPTH

surface of water

Depth (n negative centimeters)

Drop Site (cm)

QUESTIONS:

1. How does your test-point ocean floor compare to the actual graph of all the points on the ocean floor? _____

_____

2. How might making too few measurements affect the conclusions you might draw about the shape of the ocean floor (or any other investigation)? _____

_____

3. How has the use of sonar aided the study of the ocean floor? _____

_____

4. Imagine that you were actually in a boat trying to map the ocean floor like you did in this investigation. What are some possible things that could happen to "mess up" your measurement accuracy?

a. _____

b. _____

Date: _____   Names: _____

DENSITY OF SOLUTIONS

INTRODUCTION: When you put a pot of water on the stove burner, what causes the whole pot of water to get hot instead of just the water at the bottom of the pot?

OBJECTIVE: In the ocean, deep water currents are driven by three major forces: density, salinity, and temperature. Colder, more dense, or saltier solutions sink to the bottom of the ocean, while warmer, less dense, or less salty water rises to the surface of the ocean. Such circulation is responsible for the mixing of ocean waters. We will investigate the effects of density in this activity.

PROCEDURE:

1. Stick your short straw into the potato section at a 45° angle to hold the straw up. If your potato leaks because the straw is placed too deep, remove the straw and insert it again someplace else.
2. You have been provided 4 different-colored, different-density solutions.
3. It is your job to determine the layering order of the solutions by placing about a finger's width of each, drop by drop, into the straw without mixing them so that the most dense solution will go to the bottom.
4. Choose a color and place it in the straw. Label the color in "Trial 1" below.
5. Repeat with the next color.
6. If mixing occurs, abort that trial and start a new trial, beginning with a different color and labeling a different trial straw in the diagrams below.
7. When you have determined the order of density, dump used liquids in your "waste" container. **Do not contaminate your colored solutions by dumping waste into them or by using droppers for more than one solution.**

DATA: (Y = YELLOW, G= GREEN, B = BLUE, R = RED)

Trial 1	Trial 2	Trial 3	Trial 4	Trial 5	Trial 6	Trial 7	Trial 8	Trial 9	Trial 10

Trial 11	Trial 12	Trial 13	Trial 14	Trial 15	Trial 16	Trial 17	Trial 18	Trial 19	Trial 20

Date: _____ Names: _____

QUESTIONS:

1. In which order did you find the solutions layered (from bottom to top)? _____

_____

2. Why do you think this order occurred? _____

_____

_____

3. If these materials were added to the ocean, which would settle to the bottom:

    1st? _____   2nd? _____

    3rd? _____   4th? _____

4. The water warmed at the bottom of a pot of water would become less dense and do what?

_____

5. Cooler water at the top of the pot would then do what? _____

_____

** The following questions will help you understand density. **

6. Which is heavier, 1 gram of lead or 1 gram of feathers? _____

Why? _____

_____

7. Which is heavier, 1 cup of lead or 1 cup of feathers? _____

Why? _____

_____

Date: _____ Names: _____

SALINITY OF SOLUTIONS

INTRODUCTION: If you buy an "Icee" or "Slurpy" beverage, where does all of the flavor end up as you drink it?

OBJECTIVE: In the ocean, deep currents of water are driven by three major forces: density, salinity, and temperature. Colder, more dense, or saltier solutions sink to the bottom of the ocean, while warmer, less dense, or less salty water rises to the surface of the ocean. Such circulation is responsible for the mixing of ocean waters. We will investigate the effects of salinity in this activity.

PROCEDURE:

1. Stick your straw into the potato section at a 45° angle to hold the straw up. If your potato leaks because the straw is placed too deeply, remove the straw and insert it again someplace else.
4. You have been provided with 4 different-colored, different-salinity solutions.
3. It is your job to determine the layering order of the solutions by placing about a finger's width of each, drop by drop, into the straw without mixing them, so that the saltiest solution will go to the bottom.
4. Choose a color and place it in the straw. Label the color in "Trial 1" below.
5. Repeat with the next color.
6. If mixing occurs, abort that trial and start a new trial, beginning with a different color and labeling a different trial straw in the diagrams below.
7. When you have determined the order of salinity, dump used liquids in your "waste" container. **Do not contaminate your colored solutions by dumping waste into them or by using droppers for more than one solution.**

DATA: (Y = YELLOW, G = GREEN, B = BLUE, R = RED)

Trial 1	Trial 2	Trial 3	Trial 4	Trial 5	Trial 6	Trial 7	Trial 8	Trial 9	Trial 10

Trial 11	Trial 12	Trial 13	Trial 14	Trial 15	Trial 16	Trial 17	Trial 18	Trial 19	Trial 20

Date: _____ Names: _____

QUESTIONS:

1. In which order did you find the solutions layered (from bottom to top)?_____

_____

2. Why do you think this order occurred? _____

_____

3. If these materials were added to the ocean, which would settle to the bottom:

    1st? _____   2nd? _____

    3rd? _____   4th? _____

4. Where in the ocean would the saltiest water be located? _____

Least salty? _____

Marbles   **Marbles and Salt**

Look at the diagram above. The marbles represent water molecules. The salt represents anything that will dissolve in water. Notice that salt is added, but the level of the marbles does not change.

5. Why doesn't the level of the marbles (water) change when something is "dissolved" in it?

_____

_____

_____

6. How would the density of solutions with and without substances dissolved in them differ?

_____

_____

Date: _____ Names: _____

SALTY SITUATIONS

INTRODUCTION: If you heat water in a pot on the stove, adding salt just before it boils does what to the water? What happens if you try to freeze salty water? Does it freeze as quickly as tap water?

OBJECTIVE: Dissolving substances in a liquid changes the properties of the liquid. Such changes can affect the boiling point, freezing point, or the rate at which the temperature of the substance changes. In this activity, we will investigate how adding salt to water affects the boiling point, freezing point, and rate of temperature change of water.

PROCEDURE: <u>Heating Water</u>
    1. Measure 40 mL of water and put it into your 250-mL beaker.
    2. Place the thermometer in the beaker, and allow about 30 seconds for it to adjust. Measure the starting temperature of the water, and record it in the chart.
    3. Heat the water for 7 minutes—measuring the temperature every minute and recording each temperature in the chart.
    4. Remove the beaker from the heat with tongs and dump out the water.

<u>Heating Salt Water</u>
1. Measure 40 mL of water and put it into your 250-mL beaker.
2. Add 2 teaspoons of salt to the beaker of water.
3. Repeat steps 2–4 from "Heating Water" above.

<u>Cooling Water</u>
1. Measure 40 mL of water and put it into your 250-mL beaker.
2. Place the thermometer in the beaker, and allow 30 seconds for it to adjust. Measure the starting temperature of the water, and record it in the chart.
3. Add 2–3 ice cubes to the water.
4. As the water cools, measure the temperature every minute for 7 minutes and record it in the chart.
5. Dump the ice water into the sink.

<u>Cooling Salt Water</u>
1. Measure 40 mL of water and put it into your 250-mL beaker.
2. Add 2 teaspoons of salt to the water, stir, and measure its starting temperature and record it in the chart.
3. Repeat steps 3–5 from "Cooling Water" above.

** GRAPH ALL DATA ON THE GRAPH ON THE NEXT PAGE. USE THE FOLLOWING LINES TO REPRESENT EACH TYPE OF WATER:

—————— Heated Water   ▪ ▪ ▪ ▪ ▪ ▪ ▪ Cooled Water
- - - - - - - - - - - Heated Salt Water   ● ● ● ● ● ● ● Cooled Salt Water

Date: _____ Names: _____

SOLUTION	TEMPERATURE OF SOLUTION AT EACH ONE-MINUTE INTERVAL							
	Start	1	2	3	4	5	6	7
Heated Water								
Heated Salt Water								
Cooled Water								
Cooled Salt Water								

SALT EFFECTS ON HEATING AND COOLING OF WATER

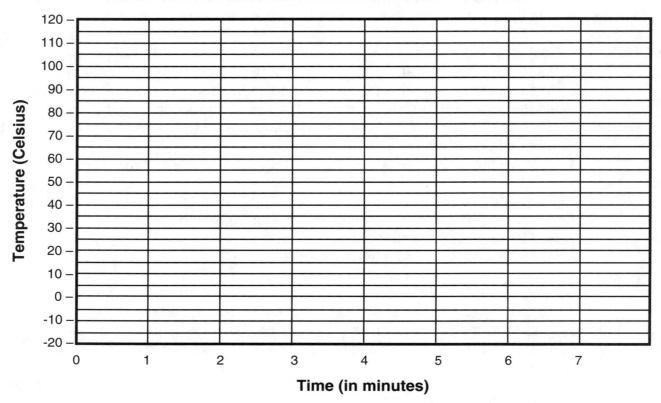

QUESTIONS:

1. How much does the temperature of water increase in 7 minutes while heating? _____

2. How much does the temperature of salt water increase in 7 minutes while heating? _____

3. What effect does a dissolved substance have on the boiling point of a liquid? _____

_____

4. How much does the temperature of water decrease in 7 minutes while cooling? _____

5. How much does the temperature of salt water decrease in 7 minutes while cooling? _____

6. What effect does a dissolved substance have on the cooling of a liquid? _____

_____

Date: _____ Names: _____

SALINITY TESTING

INTRODUCTION: How salty is ocean water? How can you figure out how much salt is in water?

OBJECTIVE: The amount of salt that is dissolved in a liquid affects the density of the liquid, causing objects to float at different levels in solutions of different salinity. In this activity, we will construct devices called HYDROMETERS that can be used to estimate salt content in liquid. We will then use the hydrometers to estimate the salt content of three test solutions.

PROCEDURE: SET-UP
1. Check the plugs on the bottom of your 3 straws.
2. Put 200 mL of tap water into your 250-mL beaker.
3. Put the plugged straws into the water—plug end down. If the straws do not float "standing up" in the water, add metal beads (about 14) to the straws until they do.

CALIBRATION
4. While the straws are floating in the water, adjust the small rubber bands on the straws so that they are at the surface level of the water.
5. Remove the straws from the water and measure the distance from the black rings to the BOTTOM (plugged end) of the straws. Record these distances (**in millimeters**) in the chart below.
6. Find the average of the 3 distances.
7. Repeat steps 4 and 5 for each of the 3 different concentrations of salt water.
   a. For each concentration listed in the chart below, use the following recipe to mix the solutions not provided:
      50% = 100 mL saturated water + 100 mL tap water
      25% = 100 mL 50% solution + 100 mL tap water
   c. Place the three hydrometers in the solution, and adjust the rings to the water surface.
   d. Remove the hydrometers from the water and measure the distances between the rings and bottoms of the straws. Record measurements in the chart below.
8. **Graph calibrated results in the graph on page 78.**

SALT CONCENTRATION	FLOATING HEIGHTS (MILLIMETERS)			
	Straw #1	Straw #2	Straw #3	Average
Plain Water (0%)				
Saturated with Salt (100%)				
Half Saturated (50%)				
One-fourth Saturated (25%)				

Date: _____ Names: _____

TEST SOLUTIONS

9. Use your calibrated hydrometers (straws) to estimate the salt concentration of the 3 solutions at the front of the room by following these steps:

    a. Place your 3 hydrometers in one of the solutions up front.

    b. Adjust the black rings.

    c. Remove the hydrometers from the solution, and measure the distance from the ring to the bottom of the straw.

    d. Record these numbers in the chart below and average them.

    e. Use this average to predict the salt concentration of each test solution by comparing it to your calibrated averages.

    f. Repeat for the other 2 test solutions.

SOLUTION	FLOATING HEIGHTS (MILLIMETERS)				
	Straw #1	Straw #2	Straw #3	Average	Salt Concentration
TEST 1					
TEST 2					
TEST 3					

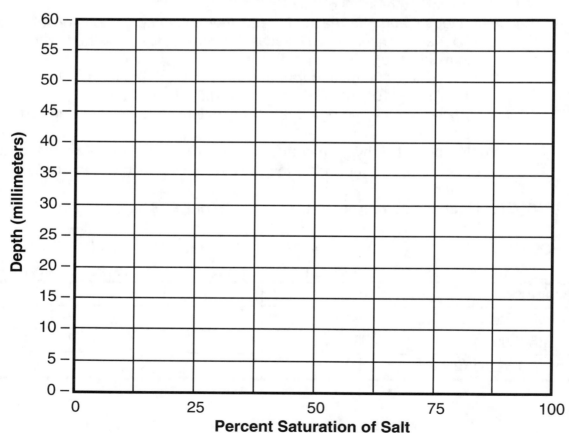

DEPTH VERSUS PERCENT SATURATION OF SALT

Depth (millimeters) vs. Percent Saturation of Salt

Date: _____ Names: _____

QUESTIONS:

1. How does the concentration of salt in a solution affect the floating height of your hydrometer?

_____

_____

2. Based on your data, where is it a little easier to float, in a lake or in the ocean? _____

_____

3. Based on your graphed data, what would be the floating height of a straw (hydrometer) in a solution that is:

     a. 75% saturated? _____

     b. 12.5 % saturated? _____

4. Based on your graphed data, what would be the percent of saturation of a solution in which your hydrometer floated at a height of:

     a. 43 mm? _____

     b. 41 mm? _____

     c. 39 mm? _____

Date: ____ _____   Names: _____

DAVEY JONES'S LOCKER

INTRODUCTION: How heavy would something have to be to float on water, be suspended in water, or sink to the bottom of water?

OBJECTIVE: There is a pirate's myth that all the nonmetal treasures and dead bodies from sunken ships are floating at some magic level in the ocean depths. This level has been named after a pirate as Davey Jones's Locker.

PROCEDURE:
1. We will need to construct an "ocean" of different densities.
2. Do this by adding the colder, more dense, blue solution to the first 25 mL of your graduated cylinder.
3. Very gently pipette (drop by drop) the next 25 mL of warmer, less dense, yellow solution on top of the blue. (A good set-up has almost no green area where mixing has occurred.)
4. We will next investigate the mass (in number of pellets) of objects that float in:
   a. the upper section just below the surface,
   b. at the junction of the two layers, and
   c. in the bottom layer just above the bottom of the graduated cylinder.
5. A vial will be used to carry the cargo (pellets).
6. Begin the investigation by adding a few pellets to the vial and testing its flotation. Try to get the vial to float in the upper section. If the vial floats above the surface, remove it and add more pellets. If the vial drops to the junction of the colors, remove it and take out some of the pellets.
7. When you reach a number of pellets that floats the vial at just the right height, you have succeeded.
8. Repeat this process for the other two levels. Record the number of pellets in the chart below.
9. Plot the data on the bar graph by coloring in a bar above each level to show the number of pellets.

WATER LEVEL	NUMBER OF PELLETS (MASS)
Top Level	
Junction	
Bottom Level	

Graph y-axis: 50, 45, 40, 35, 30, 25, 20, 15, 10, 5, 0
Graph x-axis: Top   Junction   Bottom

Date: _____ Names: _____

QUESTIONS:

1. How many pellets were needed to float the vial at each level:

      a. Top? _____

      b. Junction? _____

      c. Bottom? _____

2. What would happen to metal objects lost in shipwrecks? Why? _____

_____

_____

3. Based on your graphed data, how many pellets are needed to float the vial HALFWAY BETWEEN:

      a. the top level and the junction? _____

      b. the junction and the bottom level? _____

Date: _____ Names: _____

HEAT CAPACITY OF SAND AND WATER

INTRODUCTION: When you are at the beach, which way does the wind blow when it is really hot during the day? Which way does it blow at night?

OBJECTIVE: As materials absorb energy from sunlight, they warm. The air above them warms, and as the air molecules warm, they move faster, bumping together at greater velocities and bouncing farther away. This causes the warmer air to become less dense and rise. As air rises, more air must "blow in" from nearby to take its place, thus resulting in a breeze.

PROCEDURE:
1. Measure 200 mL of sand and place it in one styrofoam cup.
2. Measure 200 mL of water and place it in another styrofoam cup.
3. Measure a starting temperature for each cup and record it in the chart below.
4. Using a ring stand, position the light source 30 cm above the two cups. (You may have four cups here since you may be sharing the light with the group next to you.)
5. Allow the cups to warm beneath the light for the next 10 minutes.
6. Every minute take a temperature reading of each cup and record it in the chart.
7. After 10 minutes, remove the cups from the light source (or turn off the light) and continue taking temperature readings for an additional 10 minutes as the cups cool.
8. Record these cooling temperatures in the chart.
9. At the end of the second 10 minutes, graph all of the temperatures using different lines for the water (-------) and the sand (————).

TEMPERATURES (Celsius)

CUP	START	HEATING										COOLING									
		1	2	3	4	5	6	7	8	9	10	11	12	13	14	15	16	17	18	19	20
Sand																						
Water																						

QUESTIONS:

1. Which substance warmed most? _____

2. Which substance cooled most? _____

3. After a hot day at the beach, which would cool fastest at night? _____

_____

Date: _____ Names: _____

4. Use the information in the "Objective" and from your results to answer the following:

      a. During a hot day at the beach, which direction would the breeze at the beach blow? Why?

_____

_____

      b. At night after a hot day at the beach, which direction would the breeze at the beach blow? Why?

_____

_____

5. What characteristic of oceans probably affects the climates of coastal regions most? Why?

_____

_____

_____

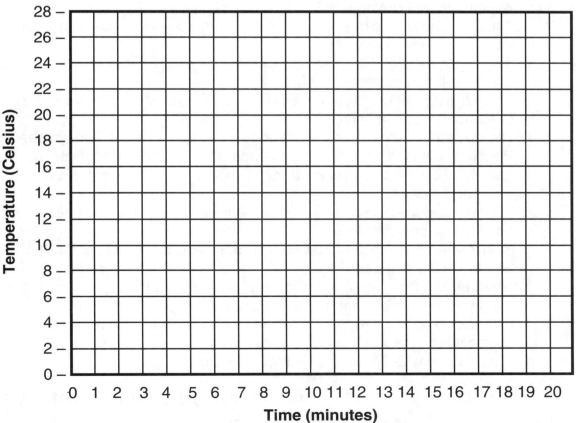

TEMPERATURE VERSUS TIME

Date: _____ Names: _____

SURFACE CURRENTS

INTRODUCTION: If you threw a bottle into the ocean off the east coast of the United States, where would it be carried to? What if you threw it into the ocean off the west coast?

OBJECTIVE: Surface currents in the oceans are caused by three major types of winds: POLAR EASTERLIES, PREVAILING WESTERLIES, AND TRADE WINDS. Trade winds occur on either side of the equator. Polar easterlies occur at each pole. Prevailing westerlies occur between the polar easterlies and trade winds. In this activity, we will examine the effect of some of these wind systems on surface currents in the oceans.

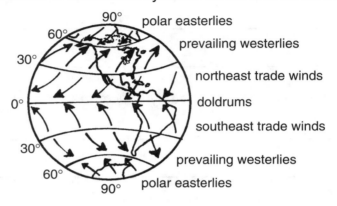

PROCEDURE:
1. Lay a laminated map as flatly as possible on the bottom of the pan provided.
2. For each map provided, you will need to construct the portion of its coastline that appears in the "dotted box."
3. The coastline should be constructed by rolling 2 chunks of clay into long ropes and flattening them slightly.
4. Construct the coastline by shaping the clay ropes into the outlines of each coastline in the dotted box in Map 1.
5. Press the clay onto the laminated paper so that it seals the clay to the paper, but does not flatten the clay.
6. The clay outline should reach from one side of the pan to the other (not end to end).
7. Pour the AQ–1000 into the ocean space between the clay outlines. (It should be held there by the clay outlines and the slight curve of the laminated paper at the sides of the pan.)
8. You will produce the wind for each experiment by blowing through a straw with a continuous, steady exhale.
9. Hold the straw above the arrow on each map, about 4–6 inches from the liquid and at about a 45° angle.
10. After blowing the "wind" in the correct direction over the "ocean" for 1–2 minutes, you will be able to observe the surface current resulting.
11. On each respective map, draw arrows with a wax pencil to represent the surface current produced by your wind system.
12. Repeat steps 2–11 for each additional map.

** DO NOT POUR YOUR AQ–1000 DOWN THE DRAIN!! RETURN IT TO ITS CONTAINER AT YOUR LAB STATION. **

84

Date: _____ Names: _____

MAP 1: Northeast Tradewinds (Atlantic Coast)

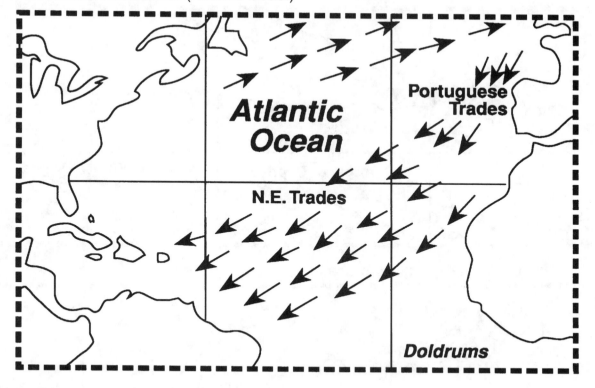

MAP 2: Southeast Tradewinds (Atlantic Coast)

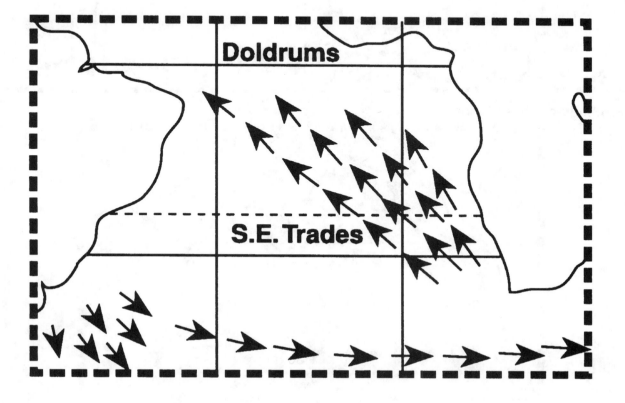

Date: _____   Names: _____

MAP 3: Northeast Tradewinds (Pacific Coast)

MAP 4: Southeast Tradewinds (Pacific Coast)

MAP 5: Indian Ocean Monsoons

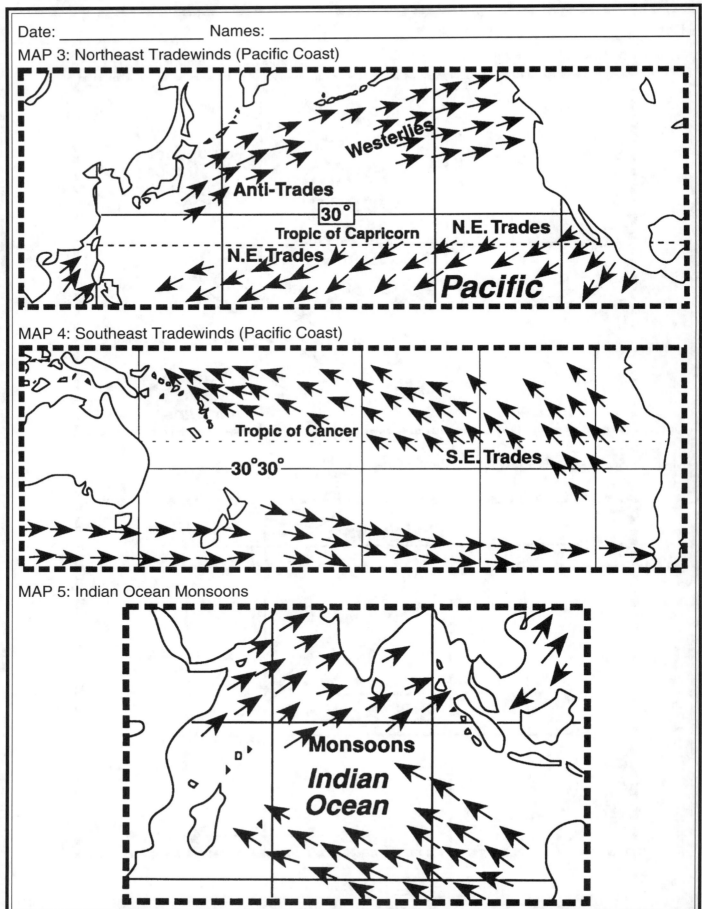

Date: _____ Names: _____

QUESTIONS:

1. What changes the direction of surface currents more than anything else?

_____

_____

_____

2. If a sealed bottle with a note in it were placed into a surface current off of North Carolina, what

country/continent would it likely reach next? _____

After that? _____

After that? _____

After that? _____

3. How might these surface currents and prevailing winds be used for fuel-efficient travel?

_____

_____

_____

_____

Date: _____ Names: _____

WATER CYCLE TALES

INTRODUCTION: Imagine that you are a droplet of water vapor in the air. What would have to happen to you in order for you to become water in a lake?

OBJECTIVE: In this activity, each individual/group will create a water droplet character and then describe what happens to this character through steps of the water cycle.

REQUIREMENTS:
1. Name the water droplet character.
2. Use at least 3 steps in the water cycle.
3. Write enough to fill this page.
4. Illustrate your water droplet (in its adventures, preferably) on a separate sheet of paper.
5. We will use the last 10 minutes of class time to share our tales.

_____

_____

_____

_____

_____

_____

_____

_____

_____

_____

_____

_____

_____

_____

_____

_____

_____

OCEANOGRAPHY ANSWER KEYS

WATER: THE MICKEY MOUSE MOLECULE (page 63)
1. Protons are in the nucleus. Neutrons are in the nucleus. Electrons are in energy levels or electron shells outside the nucleus.
2. First energy level: 2; second energy level: 8
3. The two hydrogens and one oxygen share two electrons.
4. There is an accumulation of electrons at one end resulting in a negative charge there, and there are two positive hydrogen protons at the opposite end.
5. Water molecules look like Mickey Mouse faces.

WATER ACTIVITIES (page 65–66)
This is an exploratory activity, and answers will depend on student data.

SURFACE TENSION (page 68)
1. Answer depends on student data.
2. The container with the largest opening should hold the most coins.
3. The larger the opening, the more coins it will hold.
4. Answers will vary but may include things such as: a. insects walk on water; b. flat aluminum foil will float, but it sinks when balled up; c. lily pads float on water; and d. water spilled on counters will bead up.

ROCK BOTTOM (page 70)
1. Answer depends on student data, but usually test points give much less accurate information than the actual graph.
2. You might miss major trenches or seamounts if you take too few measurements.
3. Sonar makes mapping the seafloor faster, more accurate, and much easier.
4a. Wave movement up and down makes measurement difficult.
  b. Currents may drag weights sideways and cause longer measurements.

DENSITY OF SOLUTIONS (page 72)
1. Answers depend on set-up colors. Order is from bottom to top: glycerine, salt water, water, and alcohol.
2. Glycerine is most dense, while alcohol is least dense.
3. 1st: glycerine; 2nd: salt water; 3rd: water, 4th: alcohol.
4. The warm water would then rise to the top of the pot.
5. Cooler water then sinks to the bottom of the pot.
6. Neither, both weigh 1 gram.
7. One cup of lead, because lead is more dense.

SALINITY OF SOLUTIONS (page 74)
1. Answers depend on set-up colors. Saturated salt water goes to the bottom followed by 50% saturated water, then 25% saturated water, and finally tap water on top.
2. Saturated water is more dense because dissolved salt fills the spaces between water molecules.
3. 1st: 100% saturated; 2nd: 50%; 3rd: 25%; 4th: tap water.
4. The saltiest water is on the bottom and the freshest water is at the top.
5. Dissolved materials fill spaces between molecules.
6. When spaces between molecules are filled with dissolved substances, the density increases.

SALTY SITUATIONS (page 76)
1. Answer depends on student data.
2. Answer depends on student data.
3. Dissolved salt increases the boiling point of water.
4. Answer depends on student data.
5. Answer depends on student data.
6. Dissolved salt decreases the freezing point of water.

SALINITY TESTING (page 79)
1. The hydrometer will float higher in more salty solutions.
2. It will be easier to float in the ocean than in a lake.
3a. and b. will be based on student data.
4a., b., and c. will be based on the graph of student data.

DAVEY JONES'S LOCKER (page 81)
1a., b., and c answers will depend on student data.
2. Metal objects will sink to the bottom of the ocean because they are more dense than salt water.
3a. and b. answers are based on the graph of student data.

HEAT CAPACITY OF SAND AND WATER (page 82–83)
1. Sand should warm most.
2. Sand should cool most.
3. Sand should cool fastest at night.
4a. Day: On a hot day at the beach, the wind should blow from the water onto the beach. As hot sand warms air above it, the air rises and a breeze from the water blows in to replace it.
  b. Night: At night after a hot day, the wind would blow from the sand to the water. The sand cools faster and the water stays warm longer. Air above the water is warmed and rises, and the air from the coast blows out to replace it.
5. They cool less quickly than the sand of the beaches, and the reactions described in 4a. and b. take place.

SURFACE CURRENTS (page 87)
1. Winds and landmasses affect current directions most.
2. Iceland, then Europe, then Africa, then South America.
3. If you were familiar with the surface currents, you could plan ocean travel to ride the currents.

WATER CYCLE TALES (page 88)
This is a creative writing experience. Check for the inclusion of steps in the water cycle.

METEOROLOGY INDEX AND MATERIALS LIST

PERCENT OF OXYGEN IN AIR 92
Birthday candles, wax or clay, penny, water, petri dish, graduated cylinder, marker.

THE PRESSURE IS ON 94
Two balloons, meterstick, string, straight pin, index card, cup, water, aluminum soft-drink can, heat source, large pan filled with cold water, beaker tongs, graduated cylinder.

UNDER PRESSURE 96
Fettuccini noodles, metric ruler, softball, bathroom (toilet) tissue. This actually works best on a larger scale using balsa wood and newspapers.

RADIATION AND HEAT ABSORPTION (INDOORS) 98
Strips that are made of different colors of laminated construction paper fastened together into "pockets," thermometers, heat lamps (or a sunny day), a timing device, and colored pencils.

RADIATION AND HEAT ABSORPTION (OUTDOORS) 100
Same as above, except cups of paint-colored water are used instead of construction paper pockets. Tempera paints in the colors listed, clear cups, squares of aluminum foil, and teaspoons are needed.

THE CORIOLIS EFFECT 102
Round balloon and marker.

MEASURING DEW POINT 104
250-mL beaker, water, ice, and a thermometer.

WEATHER MAKERS 106
400-mL beaker, metal spoon, heat source, teaspoon, salt, water, test tubes, and ice cubes.

WINDCHILL FACTOR 108
Water, salt water, alcohol, glycerine, four droppers, filter paper, thermometers, rubber bands, and windchill chart.

RELATIVE HUMIDITY AND HEAT INDEX 111
Three thermometers, cotton cloth (or sling psychrometers), water, and relative humidity and heat index charts.

HOT AIR BALLOONS 114
Seven sheets of tissue paper (30" X 20"), 20 inches of wire, meterstick, tape, and scissors. See pages 115–116 for folding diagrams.

ANSWER KEYS 117

Date: _____   Names: _____

PERCENT OF OXYGEN IN AIR

INTRODUCTION: When you breathe deeply, are you breathing in oxygen? How much of the air
that you breathe is made up of oxygen?

OBJECTIVE: The air is made up of a mixture of gases. Nitrogen and oxygen are the most abundant
of those gases. Oxygen is used to form minerals on the earth's surface, for animal
respiration, and in the burning of fuels. In this investigation, we will experiment to
determine the percent of oxygen in air as it is burned up during combustion (by fire).

PROCEDURE:
1. Light your candle.
2. Put a drop of wax on the penny provided and stick the bottom of the candle onto
the penny. Blow out the candle and set it in the flat petri dish provided.
3. Fill the test tube provided full (level to the top) of water, then pour the water into
a graduated cylinder to measure the volume of the water in the test tube. Record
this volume in the chart below as "Original Volume."
4. Pour this water into the petri dish and dry the outside of the test tube.
5. Re-light the candle and **quickly** put the upside-down test tube over the burning
candle so that the **mouth of the test tube is under water.**
6. As the flame burns and oxygen is used, the water will rise into the test tube to fill
the space left by the oxygen.
7. When the candle burns out, mark the level of the water on the test tube with the
marker provided.
8. To figure the volume of the oxygen used, fill the test tube to the mark (this is the
amount of air in the upside-down test tube), find the volume, and subtract this
volume from the original volume to find the oxygen volume (volume of oxygen
burned and replaced by water).
9. Repeat for 2 more trials, and record this data in the chart below.
10. **Calculate "Percent Oxygen"** by dividing the "Volume Oxygen" by the "Original
Volume" and multiplying by 100.

$$\frac{\textbf{Volume Oxygen}}{\textbf{Original Volume}} \textbf{ X 100 = Percent Oxygen}$$

11. Total and average the "Percent Oxygen" for the 3 trials.

TRIAL #	ORIGINAL VOLUME	– VOLUME OF WATER	= VOLUME OXYGEN	PERCENT OXYGEN
1				
2				
3				
			TOTAL:	
			AVERAGE:	

Date: _____ Names: _____

QUESTIONS:

1. What does the candle flame do? _____

_____

_____

_____

2. Why does water go up into the test tube as the candle burns/burns out? _____

_____

_____

_____

3. How might the percent of oxygen vary from a greenhouse (filled with plants) to a bag filled with

air exhaled by you? _____

_____

_____

_____

4. How would your percent of oxygen calculation be different if you:

    a. used a larger test tube? _____

_____

_____

    b. used a larger candle? _____

_____

_____

Date: _____ Names: _____

THE PRESSURE IS ON

INTRODUCTION: As you walk around, you support a column of air on your shoulders that goes all the way to the top of the atmosphere. How can you prove that this air pressure is pushing down on you?

OBJECTIVE: The air has weight, yet we do not notice it. Everyone must hold up the weight of the air on top of him or her (all the way to the top of the atmosphere). Every object must support all of the air on top of it, or it will collapse. Therefore, AIR PRESSURE is a force that can push downward on things on the earth.

Air pressure can also act in other directions. Temperature has a great deal of effect on this type of air pressure force. When air is warm, it is less dense, and the same amount of air takes up more space (molecules spread apart and pressure is lower). When air is cold, it is more dense, and the same amount of air takes up less space (molecules are closer together and pressure is higher). In each of these cases, the mass (weight) of the air does not change; only its volume (amount of space it takes up) changes. In these activities, we will examine some examples of these two concepts.

I. AIR HAS WEIGHT

PROCEDURE:
1. Inflate your 2 balloons to a relatively large size. Both balloons should be about the same size.
2. Tie the balloons to opposite ends of a meterstick.
3. In **one** balloon, pinch a section of the balloon together and place a tiny pinhole in the balloon. This should be done on one end of the balloon or the other so that it does not explode.
4. With a third string, suspend the meterstick near its middle so that it hangs perfectly level. You may need to slide the hanging string toward one end or the other.
5. Hang the meterstick/balloon setup off the side of your table and leave it until you complete the next two activities.
6. After the next two activities, complete the following questions.

QUESTIONS:

1. How is your balloon system different from when you left it? _____

_____

2. How might this activity demonstrate that air has weight? _____

_____

_____

Date: _____ Names: _____

II. AIR EXERTS FORCE (Cup and index card)

PROCEDURE:
1. Fill a cup full to the rim with water.
2. Wet the index card provided.
3. Place the index card across the rim of the cup so that there are no spaces into the opening of the cup. (Cup is covered by card.)
4. **Over the sink,** hold the index card in place, slowly turn the cup and index card over (upside-down), and remove your hand.

QUESTIONS:
1. What happened when you removed your hand? _____

_____

2. What held the index card in place? _____

_____

III. TEMPERATURE AFFECTS AIR PRESSURE (Soft-drink cans collapse)

PROCEDURE:
1. Get an all-aluminum soft-drink can.
2. Rinse the can with water, and add 20 mL of water to the can.
3. Place the can on the hot plate nearest you.
4. Heat the can until steam is rapidly escaping from the can.
5. **Using the tongs provided,** grasp the can and quickly flip the can upside-down into the cold water bath provided. (You must do this quickly. If you do it too slowly, nothing will happen because the air that was forced out of the can opening may be replaced by air from the room, keeping air pressures inside and outside the can equal.

QUESTIONS:
1. What happened to the air molecules inside the can as it was heated? _____

_____

2. What happened to the hot can when it was suddenly placed in cold water? _____

_____

3. Consider the effect of temperature on air molecules (and air pressure) and describe what happened.

_____

_____

Date: _____ Names: _____

UNDER PRESSURE

INTRODUCTION: Is the weight of air enough to break thin pieces of wood or uncooked noodles?

OBJECTIVE: The air has weight, yet we do not notice it. Everyone must hold up the weight of the air on top of him or her (all the way to the top of the atmosphere). Every object must support all of the air on top of it, or it will collapse. Therefore, AIR PRESSURE is a force that can push downward on things on the earth.

Air pressure can also act in other directions. Temperature has a great deal of effect on this type of air pressure force. When air is warm, it is less dense, and the same amount of air takes up more space (molecules spread apart and pressure is lower). When air is cold, it is more dense, and the same amount of air takes up less space (molecules are closer together and pressure is higher). In each of these cases, the mass (weight) of the air does not change; only its volume (amount of space it takes up) changes.

AIR EXERTS A DOWNWARD FORCE (Noodles and tissue)

** This activity may also be done using balsa strips and newspaper for a larger-scale effect.

PROCEDURE:

1. Get 3 fettuccini noodles.

2. The noodles are 24 cm long. Measure 6 cm from one end and mark the distance.

3. Lay a fettuccini on the counter, with the marked 6 cm hanging off the edge. Drop a softball from a height of 10 cm onto the fettuccini. Record what happens in the chart below.

4. Using that same fettuccini, place the 6 cm off of the counter and place a twice-folded square of tissue at the other end of the fettuccini.

5. Drop the softball from 10 cm above onto the fettuccini. Record results in the chart.

6. Using that same fettuccini, place the 6-cm end off the counter again and cover the other end with a flat square of tissue.

7. Drop the softball from 10 cm above onto the fettuccini. Be careful not to hit the table edge with the ball. Record the results in the chart.

8. Repeat steps 2–7 with 2 more pieces of fettuccini to give you a total of 3 trials for each test.

9. In the chart on the next page record whether the noodle "flips off" or "breaks."

Date: _____ Names: _____

	FETTUCCINI ALONE	FETTUCCINI AND FOLDED TISSUE	FETTUCCINI AND FLAT TISSUE
Trial 1			
Trial 2			
Trial 3			

QUESTIONS:

1. What happened when the ball was dropped on:

    a. fettuccini alone? _____

_____

    b. fettuccini with folded tissue?_____

_____

    c. fettuccini with unfolded tissue?_____

_____

2. In general, what force caused the fettuccini to break when the ball was dropped (instead of

flipping off again)? _____

_____

_____

3. What was different about that force for the two tissue trials? _____

_____

_____

Date: _____ Names: _____

RADIATION AND HEAT ABSORPTION (INDOORS)

INTRODUCTION: If it is predicted to be 100 degrees and you know that you have to work outside, what color shirt should you choose: white or black?

OBJECTIVE: The sun is very far away from us, so the energy that is received from it is spread out fairly evenly as it reaches the earth. There are two things that affect how much of that energy is absorbed when it reaches the earth. One determinant of solar energy absorption is the angle at which the energy strikes the surface of the earth. Equatorial regions receive more direct radiation and are warmer, while polar regions receive radiation at a sharp angle, which is less intense and, therefore, cooler. The other determinant is the ability of substances to absorb heat energy. Some materials absorb heat energy more efficiently, while others reflect greater amounts of the energy. Similar materials that are different colors also absorb radiant energy differently. In this activity, we will investigate which colors absorb more radiant energy.

PROCEDURE:
1. At your lab station, you will find a laminated "pocket" of a certain color of construction paper.
2. Insert a thermometer into the color "pocket," allow about 1 minute for the temperature to stabilize, and record a starting temperature for your color in the chart.
3. Turn on the heat lamp above the color pocket.
4. Every 30 seconds, take a temperature reading of the color pocket **without removing the thermometer!** Continue this for 10 minutes.
5. Record the temperatures in the chart (for your own color).
6. This data (and that of your classmates) will be placed on the board at the end of the activity, so you can complete your chart with your classmates' data.
7. Using colored pencils, graph each temperature (**for all colors**) on the graph.

QUESTIONS:

1. Based on your data, what general effect does color have on heat absorption?_____

_____

2. Based on your data, what color(s) absorbed the most heat? _____

3. Based on your data, what color(s) should be worn in the summer to absorb the smallest amount

of heat? _____

4. What is the range of FINAL temperatures from your data? _____

5. Based on your data, what color should solar water heaters be painted in order to absorb the

maximum amount of heat?_____

6. Why should the thermometer remain in the "color pockets" while being read?_____

_____

Date: _____   Names: _____

TIME (min/sec)	RED	WHITE	ORANGE	BROWN	GREEN	YELLOW	BLUE	BLACK
Start								
0:30								
1:00								
1:30								
2:00								
2:30								
3:00								
3:30								
4:00								
4:30								
5:00								
5:30								
6:00								
6:30								
7:00								
7:30								
8:00								
8:30								
9:00								
9:30								
10:00								

TEMPERATURE VERSUS TIME

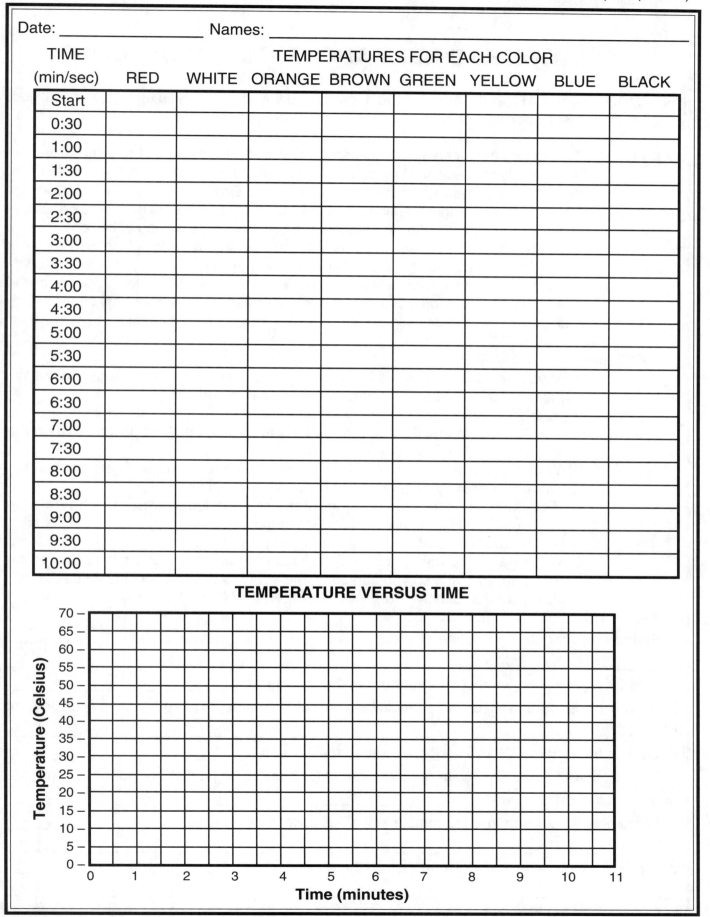

Date: _____   Names: _____

RADIATION AND HEAT ABSORPTION (OUTDOORS)

INTRODUCTION: If it is predicted to be 100 degrees and you know that you have to work outside, what color shirt should you choose: white or black?

OBJECTIVE: The sun is very far away from us, so the energy that is received from it is spread out fairly evenly as it reaches the earth. There are two things that affect how much of that energy is absorbed when it reaches the earth. One determinant of solar energy absorption is the angle at which the energy strikes the surface of the earth. Equatorial regions receive more direct radiation and are warmer, while polar regions receive radiation at a sharp angle, which is less intense and, therefore, cooler. The other determinant is the ability of substances to absorb heat energy. Some materials absorb heat energy more efficiently, while others reflect greater amounts of the energy. Similar materials of different colors also absorb radiant energy differently. In this activity, we will investigate which colors absorb more radiant energy.

PROCEDURE:
1. At your lab station, you will find a particular color of paint. Add 1 teaspoon of this paint to 100 mL of water in the clear plastic cup and stir.
2. Insert a thermometer into the colored water, allow about 1 minute for the temperature to stabilize, and record a starting temperature for the color in the chart.
3. Take the cup outside and sit it on an aluminum foil square (to exaggerate the warming effect by reflecting light back into the liquid).
4. Every minute, take a temperature of the colored liquid **without removing the thermometer!** Continue this for 20 minutes.
5. Record the temperatures in the chart (for your own color).
6. This data (along with that of your classmates) will be placed on the board at the end of the activity, so you can complete your chart with your classmates' data.
7. Using colored pencils, graph each temperature (**for all colors**) on the graph.

QUESTIONS:

1. Based on your data, what general effect does color have on heat absorption? _____
_____

2. Based on your data, what color(s) absorbed the most heat? _____

3. Based on your data, what color(s) should be worn in the summer to absorb the smallest amount of heat? _____

4. What is the range of FINAL temperatures from your data? _____

5. Based on your data, what color should solar water heaters be painted in order to absorb the maximum amount of heat? _____

6. Why should the thermometers remain in the liquid while being read? _____
_____

7. Why did we put aluminum foil underneath the cups? _____
_____

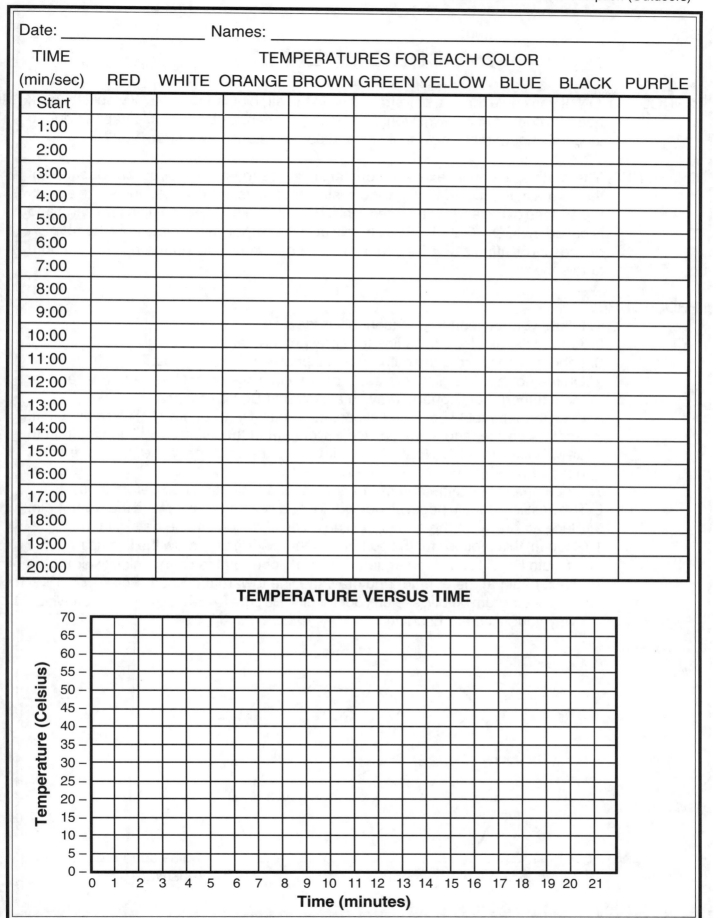

Date: _____ Names: _____

TIME (min/sec)	RED	WHITE	ORANGE	BROWN	GREEN	YELLOW	BLUE	BLACK	PURPLE
Start									
1:00									
2:00									
3:00									
4:00									
5:00									
6:00									
7:00									
8:00									
9:00									
10:00									
11:00									
12:00									
13:00									
14:00									
15:00									
16:00									
17:00									
18:00									
19:00									
20:00									

TEMPERATURE VERSUS TIME

Temperature (Celsius) vs Time (minutes)

Date: _____ Names: _____

THE CORIOLIS EFFECT

INTRODUCTION: If you could throw a ball straight up in the air, high enough that it would take six hours to come back down, would it land in your hands? What would happen during those six hours that would make it land some distance away from you?

OBJECTIVE: The earth spins on its axis in a counterclockwise (eastward) direction. Because of this rotation, the movement of wind systems, rockets, hurricanes, and so on across the surface of the earth is affected. This effect is due to the spinning of the earth and is called the CORIOLIS EFECT. In this activity, we will investigate how the rotation of the earth affects wind system movement across the northern and southern hemispheres.

PROCEDURE:
1. Inflate your balloon to a reasonably large size.
2. Around its middle, draw a line to represent the equator.
3. Label the northern and southern hemispheres on your "globe."
4. On the northern hemisphere section, draw in a sketch of North America, and on the southern hemisphere, draw in a sketch of South America.
5. One partner should hold the balloon and rotate it in a counterclockwise direction.
6. Another partner should begin with the marker at the "North Pole" and attempt to draw a line from the North Pole half way to the equator (while the globe spins beneath).
7. Place an arrow on the end of this line so its direction can be determined.
8. The next line should begin at the equator and head halfway toward the North Pole.
9. Place an arrow on the end of the line so its direction can be determined.
10. Repeat this process for the southern hemisphere, only draw the line up from the "South Pole" toward the equator (as the globe rotates counterclockwise).
11. Next begin at the equator and draw the line toward the South Pole.
12. On the diagram below, sketch your results. Be sure to draw arrows to show which way your lines are heading.

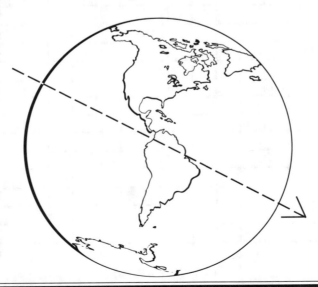

Spins counterclockwise (eastward)

Date: _____ Names: _____

QUESTIONS:

1. Wind systems that originate at the North Pole veer in what direction?

_____

2. Wind systems that originate at the equator and move northwards veer in what direction?

_____

3. Hurricanes in the northern hemisphere (near the equator) spin in what direction?

_____

4. Wind systems that originate at the South Pole veer in what direction?

_____

5. Wind systems that originate at the equator and move southwards veer in what direction?

_____

6. Hurricanes in the southern hemisphere (near the equator) spin in what direction?

_____

7. The ball that you threw in the air six hours ago is going to come down in what direction from you?

_____

Date: _____ Names: _____

MEASURING DEW POINT

INTRODUCTION: Why does a glass of iced tea "sweat"? Why is the grass sometimes wet in the morning?

OBJECTIVE: The dew point is the temperature and humidity at which water will condense out of air. You might notice this as "sweat" on the outside of a cold glass or dew on early morning grass. Warmer air can hold more water, so the humidity must be higher during warm weather to reach the dew point. Colder air requires a much lower humidity for condensation. In this activity, we will investigate the point at which dew forms at our present temperature and humidity.

PROCEDURE:

1. Fill the 250-mL beaker with 200 mL room temperature tap water.

2. Watch the outside of the beaker for the formation of condensation (sweat).

3. If condensation occurs within 2–3 minutes (it probably will not), then add warm water to your beaker and repeat until no condensation occurs within 2–3 minutes.

4. If no condensation occurs after 2–3 minutes, add 1 ice cube to the beaker and stir continuously, slowly, and gently.

5. Continue observing—wiping the outside of the beaker every 5–10 seconds to check for condensation.

6. If no condensation occurs by the time the ice cube melts, add a second cube and repeat. Continue this until condensation occurs.

7. At the second that condensation is first noticed, remove the ice cube(s) and measure the temperature. Give the thermometer about 20 seconds to stabilize.

8. Record the temperature in the chart on the next page for "Trial 1."

9. Repeat steps 1–8 for trials 2 and 3.

Date: _____ Names: _____

TRIAL NUMBER	TEMPERATURE (Celsius)
1	
2	
3	
Total:	
Average:	

10. Rising air decreases in temperature 1°C for every 100 meters in altitude. Below, subtract the dew point average calculation from the air temperature in the room. Multiply this answer by 100. This tells you to what altitude (in meters) the air in this room would need to be pushed in order to form clouds.

AIR TEMPERATURE: ____ C
DEW POINT: −____ C
____ C X 100 = _____ m
(altitude)

QUESTIONS:

1. What was the temperature of the air in the room? _____

2. What was the dew point in the room? _____

3. At what altitude would our room air form clouds? _____

4. List three examples of objects whose temperatures have reached dew point.

a. _____

b. _____

c. _____

5. Why should the ice cube be removed before taking the temperature reading?

_____

_____

6. Why is there dew on your grass in the morning and not at early evening?

_____

_____

Date: _____ Names: _____

WEATHER MAKERS

INTRODUCTION: What happens in the sky to cause it to rain or to hail?

OBJECTIVE: In order for precipitation to occur, certain conditions must be present in the atmosphere. For it to snow, the water droplets in a cloud must be at a temperature below freezing (SUPERCOOLED), there have to be enough particles of dust and pollution for water vapor to condense on, and the air temperature must be cold enough to prevent melting. For hail to form, supercooled water droplets in the clouds are necessary. As tiny particles of dust or pollution pass through this cloud (and act like nuclei for condensation or freezing to occur on), the water instantly freezes on the particles, forming hail. Rain occurs in a similar fashion, with the water vapor simply condensing on the dust or pollution particle. In this activity, we will observe models of precipitation in the forms of rain and hail.

I. MAKING RAIN

PROCEDURE:
1. Place a 400-mL beaker full of water on the heat source.
2. Heat the water until it boils or until steam rapidly rises from the beaker.
3. Hold the metal spoon in the steam flow above the beaker for 2–5 minutes.
4. Record your observations.

OBSERVATIONS: _____

_____

_____

QUESTIONS:

1. What happens when hot steam hits the cool spoon? _____

_____

2. Since there are no cold pieces of metal in the clouds, on what does water vapor collect to form raindrops?

_____

_____

Date: _____ Names: _____

II. MAKING HAIL

PROCEDURE:

1. In a 400-mL beaker, place 4 teaspoons salt.
2. Add 200 mL of water.
3. Stir to dissolve as much salt as possible. Add more salt if all 4 teaspoons dissolve.
4. Add as many ice cubes to this solution as the beaker will hold.
5. Fill 3 test tubes with water (to about 2 cm from the top **or** with about 21 mL).
6. Place the test tubes in the beaker of icy, salty water.
7. Allow this to stand undisturbed for about 10 minutes for the water in the test tubes to become supercooled (cooled past its freezing point).
8. After 10 minutes, lift one test tube from the supercooled solution.
9. Flick a tiny piece of ice downwards into the test tube.
10. Observe what happens. Record observation by "Trial 1" in the chart below.
11. Repeat the entire procedure for the two other test tubes.

OBSERVATIONS

TRIAL 1	
TRIAL 2	
TRIAL 3	

QUESTIONS:

1. Describe the conditions necessary for hail to form. _____

_____

_____

2. What effect does salt have on the ice water (why is it necessary)? _____

_____

_____

3. What happened inside the test tube when the ice pellet was dropped in?_____

_____

_____

4. What role does the ice pellet play in this reaction? _____

_____

Date: _____   Names: _____

WINDCHILL FACTOR

INTRODUCTION: Why does it feel so cold outside when it is windy? What makes windy weather so much more dangerous than cold weather with no wind?

OBJECTIVE: When a liquid evaporates, it removes heat from the material it touches. (That's why you feel cool when you get out of the pool as the water evaporates from your skin—even if it is 98°.) Your skin continuously produces moisture, so your body continuously loses heat due to evaporation. WINDCHILL describes the discomfort level that results from wind (causing increased evaporation) interacting with temperatures. In this activity, we will examine the evaporation rates of several liquids.

PROCEDURE:
1. In the cups at your lab station are 4 liquids:
    a. water
    b. salt water
    c. alcohol
    d. glycerin
2. Place a drop of each on the back of your hand to see if you can feel a "cooling sensation" due to the evaporation of the liquid.
3. Predict which liquids cause the greatest windchill due to evaporation and write them in order below:

    Greatest windchill: _____

    _____

    _____

    Least windchill: _____

4. Insert the thermometer into cup "a," and get a starting temperature.
5. Record the starting temperature in the chart.
6. Wrap the bulb of the thermometer with a small piece of filter paper and secure it with a rubber band.
7. Dip the thermometer into liquid "a," remove it (let excess drip back into cup), and record a filter temperature for liquid "a."
8. To create the wind, sling the thermometer carefully for 1 minute.
9. Record the 1-minute temperature in the chart for liquid "a."
10. Continue slinging the thermometer for another minute, and record a 2-minute temperature in the chart.
11. Repeat steps 4–10 for each of the other liquids "b–d."

Date: _____ Names: _____

CUP	LIQUID	STARTING TEMP.	FILTER TEMP.	1-MINUTE TEMP	2-MINUTE TEMP.
A	water				
B	salt water				
C	alcohol				
D	glycerin				

QUESTIONS:

1. Which liquid caused the greatest cooling? _____

The least cooling? _____

2. What process caused the cooling effect?_____

_____

3. If the air in the room was saturated with moisture, how would it affect final temperatures? Why?

_____

_____

4. Describe a weather situation in which windchill might be a concern. _____

_____

_____

5. Using the chart provided, identify the windchill if the temperatures and wind speeds are as follows:

    a. Temp. = 35 and Speed = 20 mph: _____

    b. Temp. = 20 and Speed = 30 mph: _____

    c. Temp. = 0 and Speed = 10 mph: _____

    d. Temp. = -8 and Speed = 20 mph: _____

    e. Temp. = 2 and Speed = 40 mph: _____

    f. Temp. = 29 and Speed = 35 mph: _____

    g. Temp. = 17 and Speed = 15 mph: _____

WINDCHILL TABLE

Actual Temperature	Windchill Temperature							
	Wind Speed							
	5 mph	10 mph	15 mph	20 mph	25 mph	30 mph	35 mph	40 mph
35	33	21	16	12	7	5	3	1
34	32	20	15	10	6	4	2	0
33	31	19	14	8	4	2	0	-1
32	29	18	13	7	3	1	-1	-2
31	28	17	12	5	1	-1	-3	-3
30	27	16	11	3	0	-2	-4	-4
29	26	15	9	2	-1	-4	-6	-6
28	25	13	7	0	-3	-6	-8	-8
27	23	12	5	-1	-4	-7	-9	-10
26	22	10	3	-3	-6	-9	-11	-13
25	21	9	1	-4	-7	-11	-13	-15
24	20	8	0	-5	-9	-12	-14	-16
23	19	6	-2	-6	-10	-14	-16	-18
22	18	5	-3	-7	-12	-15	-17	-19
21	17	3	-5	-8	-13	-17	-19	-21
20	16	2	-6	-9	-15	-18	-20	-22
19	15	1	-7	-11	-16	-20	-21	-23
18	14	0	-8	-12	-18	-21	-23	-25
17	14	0	-9	-14	-19	-23	-24	-26
16	13	-1	-10	-15	-21	-24	-26	-28
15	12	-2	-11	-17	-22	-26	-27	-29
14	11	-3	-12	-18	-23	-27	-29	-30
13	10	-5	-14	-20	-25	-29	-30	-32
12	9	-6	-15	-21	-26	-30	-32	-33
11	8	-8	-17	-23	-28	-32	-33	-35
10	7	-9	-18	-24	-29	-33	-35	-36
9	6	-10	-19	-26	-31	-35	-37	-38
8	5	-11	-21	-27	-32	-36	-38	-40
7	3	-13	-22	-29	-34	-38	-40	-41
6	2	-14	-24	-30	-35	-39	-41	-43
5	1	-15	-25	-32	-37	-41	-43	-45
4	0	-16	-27	-34	-39	-43	-45	-47
3	-2	-18	-28	-35	-40	-44	-47	-49
2	-3	-19	-30	-37	-42	-46	-48	-50
1	-5	-21	-31	-38	-43	-47	-50	-52
0	-6	-22	-33	-40	-45	-49	-52	-54
-1	-7	-23	-34	-41	-46	-50	-54	-56
-2	-8	-24	-36	-42	-48	-52	-55	-57
-3	-9	-25	-37	-44	-49	-53	-57	-59
-4	-10	-26	-39	-45	-51	-55	-58	-60
-5	-11	-27	-40	-46	-52	-56	-60	-62
-6	-12	-28	-41	-47	-53	-57	-61	-63
-7	-13	-29	-42	-48	-54	-59	-63	-65
-8	-13	-29	-43	-50	-56	-60	-64	-66
-9	-14	-30	-44	-51	-57	-62	-66	-68

* Temperatures are in degrees Fahrenheit.

Date: _____   Names: _____

RELATIVE HUMIDITY AND HEAT INDEX

INTRODUCTION: If you are outside working and it is really muggy, why does it feel so much hotter than the actual temperature? How does mugginess affect how hot you feel?

OBJECTIVE: The amount of moisture in the air affects how much water can evaporate into the air. The more moisture in the air, the less water that will evaporate into it. If this evaporation is from the bulb of a thermometer, then the evaporation can be measured as a temperature change. The greater the evaporation, the greater the temperature change. In this activity, we will measure the RELATIVE HUMIDITY and we will use the humidity to estimate the heat index. The HEAT INDEX is used to describe how hot it "feels" due to both temperature and humidity effects. The more humid it is the smaller the amount of evaporation from the skin and, therefore, the smaller the amount of cooling felt due to evaporation.

PROCEDURE:
1. Take your 3 thermometers outside and wait about 1 minute to get a starting temperature reading.
2. Record the starting temperature in the chart below.
3. Place the wet cotton cloth over the bulb of each thermometer.
4. Spin the thermometers in the air for 30 seconds.
5. Record the new temperatures in the chart below.
6. For each thermometer, subtract the wet bulb temperature from the dry bulb temperature.
7. To find the relative humidity:
    a. Find the dry bulb outside temperature in the left column of the chart on page 113.
    b. Find the temperature difference across the top.
    c. Go down the chart until the row and column meet. That is the relative humidity.
    d. For each set of temperatures, record the humidity in the chart below.
8. Average the 3 humidity readings by adding the 3 numbers together and dividing by 3.
9. To figure out the heat index, use the second chart on page 113 and find the humidity down the left column and the current temperature across the top.
10. Where those two numbers intersect represents the heat index.
11. Record the heat index for each humidity and temperature in the chart below.

Thermometer	Start Temp.	− Wet Bulb Temp.	= Temp. Difference	Humidity	Heat Index
1					
2					
3					
			Average Humidity:		

Date: _____ Names: _____

QUESTIONS:

1. What effect does evaporation have on temperature? _____

_____

_____

_____

2. Why do humans sweat? _____

_____

_____

_____

3. How does the amount of moisture in the air affect evaporation? _____

_____

_____

_____

4. What would the humidity be if the temperature were:

      a. 5 degrees warmer than it is today? _____

      b. 5 degrees cooler than it is today? _____

5. How does humidity affect the heat index? _____

_____

_____

_____

6. Using today's humidity reading, what would the heat index be if the temperature were:

      a. 90°? _____

      b. 95°? _____

      c. 100°? _____

RELATIVE HUMIDITY INDEX

Air Temperature	Difference Between Dry Bulb and Wet Bulb Readings										
	1	2	3	4	5	6	7	8	9	10	11
100	96	93	89	86	83	80	77	73	70	68	65
98	96	93	89	86	83	79	76	73	70	67	64
96	96	93	89	86	82	79	76	73	69	66	63
94	96	93	89	85	82	79	75	72	69	66	63
92	96	92	89	85	82	78	75	72	68	65	62
90	96	92	89	85	81	78	74	71	68	65	61
88	96	92	88	85	81	77	74	70	67	64	61
86	96	92	88	84	81	77	73	70	66	63	60
84	96	92	88	84	84	76	73	69	66	62	59
82	96	92	88	84	80	76	72	69	65	61	58
80	96	91	87	83	79	75	72	68	64	61	57
78	96	91	87	83	79	75	71	67	63	60	56
76	96	91	87	82	78	74	70	66	62	59	55
74	95	91	86	82	78	74	69	65	61	58	54
72	95	91	86	82	77	73	69	65	61	57	53
70	95	90	86	81	77	72	68	64	59	55	51

* Temperatures are in degrees Fahrenheit.

HEAT INDEX

Humidity	Temperature							
	70	75	80	85	90	95	100	105
0	64	69	73	78	83	87	91	95
10	65	70	75	80	85	90	95	100
20	66	72	77	82	87	93	99	105
30	67	73	78	84	90	96	104	113
40	68	74	79	86	93	101	110	123
50	69	75	81	88	96	107	120	135
60	70	76	82	90	100	114	132	149
70	70	77	85	93	106	124	144	
80	71	78	86	97	113	136		
90	71	79	88	102	122			
100	72	80	91	108				

* Temperatures are in degrees Fahrenheit.

Date: _____ Names: _____

HOT AIR BALLOONS

INTRODUCTION: Is it possible to build a balloon that will be light enough and large enough to fly?

OBJECTIVE: One way to demonstrate that hot air rises is to construct a hot air balloon. Because of the difference in temperatures inside and outside the balloon, the balloon will rise. Therefore, the colder the outside air the better the balloon will rise. Also, there is a critical balance between the volume of the balloon and the weight of the balloon. Therefore, it is most important that you minimize the weight of the balloon in order to get it to rise.

PROCEDURE:

1. Select 7 sheets of tissue paper. They will be used as follows:
   4 sheets will form the sides
   1 sheet will form the top
   2 sheets will be cut to form the tapered sides near the bottom

2. Put the 4 side panels aside.

3. Tapered side sections:
   a. Take the 2 bottom side sheets and stack them exactly on top of each other.
   b. Fold the stacked sheets so that they are 1/2 as long. (See figure 1.)
   c. Turn the 15″ X 20″ section so that it has the 20″ side at the bottom and fold it in half so that the 20″ side becomes 10″. (See fig. 2.)
   d. Fold again so that the 10″ side becomes 5″.
   e. Without unstacking the sheets, make a diagonal fold from the open stack of corners so that the fold goes from one corner to the other. (See fig. 2.) Press to make a clear fold.
   f. Cut off the folded section.
   g. Unfold the stacked sheets and cut them in half on the center fold so that the longest side of the tapered panel is 20″ long.

4. Now that you have 4 tapered sections, you may begin attaching them to the whole pieces that will make up the side panels.
   a. Lay the pieces out so that their ends match up. (See fig. 4.)
   b. Overlap the edges about 1/4 inch or 1/2 cm and tape along the entire length of the seam.
   c. Repeat for the other three sides.

5. Attach the sides together by overlapping their seams by about 1/4 inch or 1/2 cm and taping along the length of the seam.

6. Cut out a top from the remaining piece of tissue paper.
   a. The top should be 20″ X 20″.

Date: _____ Names: _____

7. Tape the top to the non-tapered end of the balloon. This should completely enclose the upper end of the balloon.

8. Construct a wire ring to hold the bottom of the balloon open by bending a section of wire into a circle that will fit inside the bottom of the balloon. Then fold the tissue over the wire and tape it into place.
** **Remember, minimize weight!**

PRIZES WILL GO TO: 1. FARTHEST FLYING IN EACH CLASS AND OVERALL.
                                        2. MOST CREATIVELY/BRIGHTLY DECORATED IN EACH CLASS.

BALLOON CONSTRUCTION DIRECTIONS

Figure 1: (2 sheets that will become 4 bottom panels)

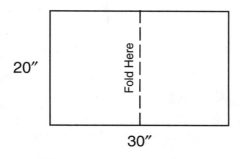

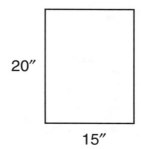

1. Fold the 2 stacked sheets along the dotted line so that the 30″ side becomes 15″.

Figure 2: (Folded sheet that will become 4 bottom panels)

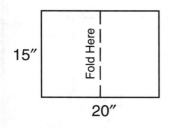 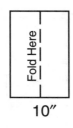 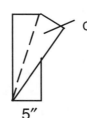 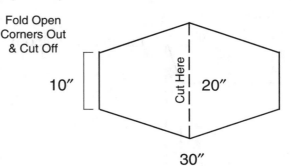

2. Turn the 15″ X 20″ section so that it has the 20″ side at the bottom.
3. Fold the section making the 20″ side become 10″.
4. Fold again so that the 10″ side becomes 5″.
5. Make a diagonal fold from the open stack of corners so that the fold goes from one corner to another, and press to make a clear fold. Cut off the folded section.
6. Unfold the stacked panels and cut them in half along the center fold so that the longest side of the tapered panel is 20″. You should now have 4 tapered panels.

Date: _____ Names: _____

BALLOON CONSTRUCTION DIRECTIONS

Figure 3:

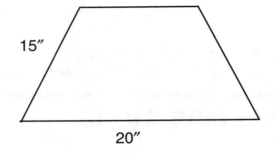

(Bottom tapered panels after cutting fold)

Figure 4:

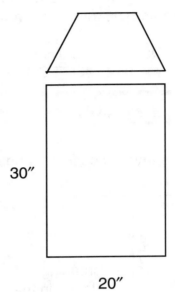

6. Attach a bottom to each side as shown.

Figure 5:

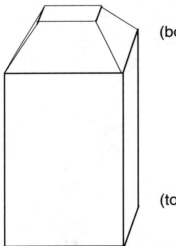

(bottom of balloon)

(top of balloon)

7. Attach all 4 side/top panels together.

Figure 6:

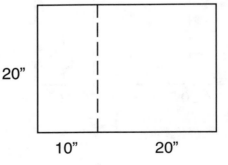

8. Cut 10″ off of the 30″ side of the top panel.
9. Attach top to 4 sides.
10. Place wire in small opening.

METEOROLOGY ANSWER KEYS

PERCENT OF OXYGEN IN AIR (page 93)
1. The flame goes out.
2. When the oxygen is burned, the air pressure in the test tube is lower, so outside air pressure pushes water into the test tube to replace the volume of oxygen burned.
3. A greenhouse would have more than the normal amount of oxygen, while a bag that is exhaled into will have less oxygen.
4a. and b. neither should affect the percentage of oxygen calculated. A larger test tube would result in a larger volume, but same percent. A larger candle would simply burn the oxygen faster.

THE PRESSURE IS ON (page 94–95)
I. 1. The balloon system has tilted so that the balloon with the hole in it is smaller and higher.
   2. The air that escaped from the smaller balloon is not in the system so the smaller balloon is now lighter.
II. 1. The index card stays in place.
   2. The air pressure in the room pushes upwards on the card and holds it in place.
III. 1. They began to move faster and some escaped.
   2. The opening is closed by the water and the air molecules in the can cool, slow down, and move closer together (decreasing the pressure inside).
3. Since the pressure is now lower in the can, the air pressure in the room crushes the can.

UNDER PRESSURE (page 97)
1a. The fettuccini should flip off the counter.
  b. The fettuccini should still flip off the counter.
  c. The fettuccini should break instead of flipping.
  ** This is difficult to achieve, so results may vary.
2. The force of the air pressure pressing down on the tissue caused the noodle to break.
3. The folded tissue weighs the same as the unfolded tissue, but the unfolded tissue had greater surface area and, therefore, greater air pressure pressing down on it.

RADIATION AND HEAT ABSORPTION (INDOORS) (page 98)
1. Answers may vary, but in general, dark colors absorb more heat.
2. Answers will depend on data.
3. Answers will vary, but in general, lighter colors should be worn.
4. Answers will be based on data.
5. Answers will be based on data.
6. Removing the thermometer from the pocket allows momentary cooling.

RADIATION AND HEAT ABSORPTION (OUTDOORS) (page 100)
1–6. Answers are the same as indoor answers above.
7. The foil reflects the sunlight back up into the cup. It reflects heat from the surface the cups are sitting on back down into the ground. This ensures that warming is due only to heat absorbed from sunlight.

THE CORIOLIS EFFECT (page 103)
1. West.
2. West.
3. Counterclockwise.
4. West.
5. West.
6. Clockwise.
7. West of you.

MEASURING DEW POINT (page 105)
1. Answer depends on student data.
2. Answer depends on data.
3. Answer depends on data.
4. Answers will vary but might include: a. a glass of cold soda "sweating"; b. moisture on car windows in the morning; c. condensation on the inside of windows on cold days.
5. You remove the ice cube so that it doesn't continue to cool the water. You want to get as close as possible to the exact temperature at the time of condensation.
6. Overnight the air temperatures cool below dew point, allowing condensation to form on the grass. Daytime temperatures rarely reach dew point because the sun is shining.

WEATHER MAKERS (page 106–107)
I. 1. Steam hits the spoon, condenses, and drips off.
   2. A small particle of dust or pollution will do the same thing that the cold spoon did.
II. 1. A supercooled temperature is needed, and condensation nuclei of dust or pollution is necessary for the water vapor to freeze on.
   2. Salt will cool the water to a temperature below freezing.
   3. The water should have frozen instantly (at least one trial and part of the way down the tube).
   4. The ice pellet acts as the condensation nuclei.

WINDCHILL FACTOR (page 109)
1. Answer depends on data, but greatest cooling was probably caused by the alcohol and least cooling by the glycerine.
2. Evaporation produced the cooling effect.
3. Not much evaporation would take place, so the temperatures would not cool much.
4. Very cold, windy, wintery days cause a great deal of concern about windchill.
5a. 12; b. -18; c. -22; d. -50; e. -50; f. -6; g. -9

RELATIVE HUMIDITY AND HEAT INDEX (page 112)
1. Evaporation produces a cooling effect.
2. Humans sweat so that the evaporation of sweat will cool them.
3. The more moisture in the air, the less evaporation occurs.
4a. and b. Both answers depend on student data.
5. As the humidity increases so does the heat index.
6a., b., and c. All answers depend on student data.

ASTRONOMY INDEX AND MATERIALS LIST

PLANETARY MOTION **120**
   One-hole stopper, 1-m string, meterstick, three pencils, and short string for elliptical orbits.

LIGHT YEARS AND STUDENT MINUTES **123**
   Timing device and trundle wheel (or long tape measure).

HOW CLOSE IS TOO CLOSE? **124**
   Meterstick, heat source, timing device, and several thermometers.

ESTIMATING DISTANCES OF FARAWAY OBJECTS **125**
   Circles cut from construction paper of 10, 20, 30, 40, 50, and 60 cm diameters, meterstick, and wooden six-sided pencil. Spotting locations should be designated by marking the areas for the students to sight from so that results can be compared.

ESTIMATING THE ALTITUDE OF OBJECTS **127**
   Quadrant (protractor with flat side taped to edge of ruler), short string, 1-hole stopper, several tall objects (listed in chart or choose your own), long tape measure, and meterstick (to measure student height to eye level).

ESTIMATING THE ANGLE OF SEPARATION OF FAR-AWAY OBJECTS **129**
   Cross-staff and nomograph (see pages 131 and 132), six color-coded strips placed at designated locations of .5, 1, 1.5, 2, 3, and 4 meters apart, and meterstick. Designate spotting locations by marking the areas to sight from so that results can be compared.

REASONS FOR THE SEASONS **133**
   Graph paper, protractor (or precut angle cards with both a 90° and 23.5° angle on each), and small flashlight.

GREENHOUSE EFFECT **135**
   Heat lamp (or sunny day outside), thermometers, two cups, soil, and plastic wrap.

GRAVITY AND ORBITAL VELOCITY OF PLANETS **137**
   Two pieces of poster paper, meterstick, marker, and calculator.

ROCKET ENGINES AND NEWTON'S THIRD LAW
   This experiment, located on page 24 in the Laboratory Skills section, may also be appropriate for use with an astronomy unit.

ANSWER KEYS **139**

Date: _____   Names: _____

PLANETARY MOTION

INTRODUCTION: When you ride a merry-go-round, do you feel like you are moving faster if you sit on the outside or if you sit halfway to the inside?

OBJECTIVE: The period of revolution for a planet is how long it takes the planet to orbit around the sun. In this activity, we will investigate how the distance a planet is from the Sun affects its period of revolution.

The orbits of the planets of the solar system are not circular, but elliptical. Generally, an ELLIPSE is formed when a curved line is drawn around two central points, the way a circle can be drawn using one central point. In our solar system, the Sun is one point, and the other does not exist. In this activity, we will examine this concept.

PROCEDURE: <u>PERIOD OF REVOLUTION</u>
1. Tie the 1-meter piece of string through the hole of the stopper.
2. Swing the stopper in an orbit above your head at a consistent speed.
3. Have a partner count 10-second time intervals while you or another partner count(s) how many times the stopper "revolved" during the 10 seconds.
4. Record your data in the chart below.
5. Repeat this procedure for a total of 3 times per length of string.
6. Total and average your data.
7. Then to calculate the number of revolutions per second, divide the average for each string length by 10. Using this, you can compare the rate at which the objects revolved at different distances.

STRING LENGTH	TRIAL 1	TRIAL 2	TRIAL 3	TOTAL	AVERAGE	REVOLUTIONS PER SECOND
100 cm						
80 cm						
60 cm						
40 cm						
20 cm						

QUESTIONS:

1. How does string length affect the number of revolutions per second? _____

_____

2. How might this idea be related to the planets orbiting the Sun?_____

_____

3. In which position on a merry-go-round are you actually traveling faster? Why? _____

_____

Date: _____ Names: _____

PROCEDURE: <u>ELLIPTICAL ORBITS</u>
1. Tie the short piece of string in a circle that is 4 cm in diameter. (Stretch the circle flat.)
2. Place the points of 2 pencils on one of the sets of dots below.
3. Drop the string loop over the 2 pencils.
4. Use a third pencil to pull the loop outwards (without moving the two other pencils), and trace the shape that the loop guides you to follow.
5. Repeat this procedure for the other two sets of dots.

TRIAL 1:

o   o

TRIAL 2:

o   o

Date: _____ Names: _____

TRIAL 3:

o   o

_ _

QUESTIONS:

1. What happens to the ellipse as the points get farther apart? _____

_____

2. Describe the evidence that our solar system might have once had two "suns"? _____

_____

_____

_____

Date: _____ Names: _____

LIGHT YEARS AND STUDENT MINUTES

INTRODUCTION: If someone was on a planet orbiting a star that is five light years away and they could look toward Earth and see us, they would see what you were doing five years ago because it would have taken five years for the light from us to reach them.

OBJECTIVE: A light year is the distance that light travels in one year. Light travels at a speed of 300,000,000 meters per second (3.0 X 10 m/sec). Because a light year is defined as the distance that light travels in one year, if a star is five light years away, then the light that you see in the sky from that star is really five years old. "Looking into space is like looking back into time." In this investigation, we will look at a similar measurement of distance: student minutes.

PROCEDURE:
1. Each member of your lab group should line up at the designated spot.
2. At the signal, you should walk toward the endpoint at a steady pace. You will be timed for 1 minute.
3. At the end of 1 minute, measure the distance that you walked and record it in the chart below. We will repeat this step twice more to get your group's average "student minute."
4. After you have calculated your individual student minute, calculate a group average by:
   a. adding the 3 average student minutes and
   b. dividing that total by 3.

PARTNER	TRIAL 1	TRIAL 2	TRIAL 3	TOTAL	AVERAGE
1					
2					
3					
				TOTAL:	
				AVERAGE:	

QUESTIONS:

1. How are student minutes similar to light years? _____
_____

2. How many student minutes are in 5,500 meters? _____

3. How many meters are in three student minutes? _____

4. You get up at 6:30, shower at 6:35, eat breakfast at 6:50, and catch the bus at 7:10.

   a. If your neighbor lives exactly 15 student minutes away from you, at what time must she leave home to catch the bus at your house? _____

   b. If student minutes were light years and your neighbor, observed you through her telescope at 6:50 her time, what would she catch you doing? _____

5. What is meant by the phrase: "Looking into space is like looking back in time"?_____

Date: _____ Names: _____

HOW CLOSE IS TOO CLOSE?

INTRODUCTION: If your dog had puppies in her doghouse during the winter, you might think about hanging a lightbulb in the doghouse to keep them warm. How low should you hang the light so that it keeps them warm but doesn't overheat them?

OBJECTIVE: Theoretically, if our solar system is made up of several planets orbiting a rather small star (our Sun), then other stars may well have planets orbiting them. Around each star there is a narrow band of temperatures at which the water that is necessary for life as we know it can exist in all three phases: solid, liquid, and gas. This temperature is called the CLEMENT ZONE. In this investigation, we will examine the location of a fake clement zone for a fake planet.

PROCEDURE:

1. The clement zone we are searching for is: _____ °C to _____ °C.
2. Set up your equipment like the diagram at the right.
3. The thermometers should be positioned on the meterstick at any place you choose. **Give the thermometers 4 minutes at each location to reach their final temperatures.**
4. After 4 minutes at a location not inside the clement zone, you may move your thermometers closer to or farther from the light in search of a distance that matches the clement zone.
5. Record your clement zone distances below as well as any other distances that you tested. **Put a rectangle around the clement zone.**

Light
0   10   20   30   40   50   60   70   80   90   100 cm

QUESTIONS:

1. What is the temperature range of our clement zone? _____°C to _____°C.

2. How far from the light source did our clement zone fall? _____ cm.

3. What happens to planets that are:

   a. closer than the clement zone? _____

   b. farther than the clement zone? _____

4. What general statement describes how distance from the radiant source (light or sun) affects

temperature? _____

Date: _____ Names:_____

ESTIMATING DISTANCES OF FARAWAY OBJECTS

INTRODUCTION: If you saw two cars in the distance and one of the cars looked a lot larger than the other, which car would you think was closer to you?

OBJECTIVE: Early astronomers did not have the equipment to bounce radio waves off of planets in order to calculate their distance from the earth. As a result, they developed a method of estimating the distance of these faraway objects by comparing their apparent sizes to the apparent sizes of objects whose distances can be measured. In this activity, we will use this method of estimation to calculate estimated distances of several objects around the school.

$$(\text{Equation}): \quad \frac{\text{diameter of object}}{\text{diameter of pencil}} = \frac{\text{distance to object}}{\text{distance to pencil}}$$

PROCEDURE:

1. Hold a standard 6-sided pencil beside a meterstick and place the end of the meterstick against your face just below your eye.
2. Point the meterstick at the object whose distance is to be measured, and move the pencil toward or away from you until the pencil just covers your view of the object.
3. Without moving the pencil, carefully read the distance between your eye and the pencil (in cm) and record in the chart below.
4. To calculate the distance to the object, multiply your observed meterstick measurement by the constant provided for you for each object.
   ** The constant has been calculated from the equation above by dividing the diameter of the object by the diameter of the pencil.
5. Repeat this for each of the objects provided, and record your results in the chart below.
6. Make sure you stand in the designated spot for each measurement.

OBJECT NUMBER	TRIAL 1	TRIAL 2	TRIAL 3	TOTAL	(AVERAGE X CONSTANT = ESTIMATED DISTANCE)	
1					14.28	
2					28.57	
3					42.86	
4					57.14	
5					71.43	
6					85.71	

Date: _____ Names: _____

QUESTIONS:

1. How would the following errors affect your results:

   a. Holding the meterstick away from your face?_____

   _____

   _____

   b. Using a fat pencil to cover the object? _____

   _____

   _____

2. Would it be possible to use something else (like your thumb) to calculate estimated distances:

   a. using the same constant you used in the activity? Why? _____

   _____

   _____

   b. using a new constant based on the diameter of your thumb? Why? _____

   _____

   _____

3. How does the distance of an object from you affect its apparent size? _____

   _____

   _____

   _____

   _____

Date: _____ Names: _____

ESTIMATING THE ALTITUDE OF OBJECTS

INTRODUCTION: If you were asked how tall the tallest tree you can see from your yard is, how could you figure out its height? Would you have to climb the tree?

OBJECTIVE: In order for early astronomers to communicate about celestial bodies, they had to be able to describe which object they were talking about. One way to do this was to describe its location. This could be done by describing its height above the horizon and its angle of separation from other well-known objects. In this activity, we will practice estimating the altitude of different objects using a "quadrant."

PROCEDURE:

1. Cut out the diagram labeled "quadrant" on the half sheet provided.
2. Using clear tape, attach the quadrant to the wooden ruler provided so that the line at 90° is even with the edge of the ruler.
3. Attach the string (with the rubber stopper as a weight on the other end) to the quadrant on the ruler so that the string attaches at the crossed lines and hangs down at 0°.
4. To use the quadrant to estimate altitude, place it in front of your eye with the top of the ruler aligned with the object to be measured.
5. Allow the string to swing freely until it stops.
6. Place a finger on the string to hold it in place on the quadrant, and check the angle shown by the string position.
7. Move forwards (to increase the angle) or backwards (to decrease the angle) until the string position is at 45°.
8. Measure your distance from the object.
9. Record this number in the chart as "Horizontal Distance."
10. Measure your height to eye level, and record this for each item as "Your Height" in the chart below.
11. The altitude of the object can then be calculated by adding your height (to eye level) to the horizontal distance.

OBJECT	YOUR HEIGHT +	HORIZONTAL DISTANCE =	ESTIMATED DISTANCE
inside ceiling			
top of school			
school bus			
electric pole			
large tree			
cafeteria ceiling			

Date: _____ Names: _____

QUESTIONS:

1. How would the following affect your calculated estimate:

    a. a breeze blowing the stopper toward your face?_____

_____

    b. a breeze blowing the stopper away from your face? _____

_____

2. How can you estimate the height of really tall objects without actually climbing and measuring them?

_____

_____

_____

✂ -

QUADRANT

Date: _____ Names: _____

ESTIMATING THE ANGLE OF SEPARATION
OF FARAWAY OBJECTS

INTRODUCTION: If you were standing in your yard and saw a UFO in the sky, how would you describe to someone else exactly where it was located?

OBJECTIVE: In order for early astronomers to communicate about celestial bodies, they had to be able to describe which object they were talking about. One way to do this was to describe its location. This could be done by describing its height above the horizon and its angle of separation from other well-known objects. In this activity, we will practice estimating the angle of separation of objects using a "cross-staff" and a chart to convert distances to angles (a NOMOGRAPH).

** In general, your hand can be used to compare your estimates as follows.
At arm's length: thumb thickness = 1 degree
                      distance from one knuckle to another = 2 degrees
                      fist width = 10 degrees
                      handspan width = 20 degrees

PROCEDURE:
1. Cut out the diagram labeled "Cross-staff" on the half sheet provided.
2. Cut along all solid lines and bend backwards along dotted lines.
3. Slide this cross-staff diagram onto the 0 end of a meterstick to construct a cross-staff.
4. Notice that there are pairs of wide, medium, and narrow notches.
5. To measure the angle between two objects, hold the cross-staff up to your eye and align the two objects just inside one pair of the notches. (Wide notches are used for objects far apart, and narrow notches are used for objects that are close together.)
6. The paper section of the cross-staff may be slid toward or away from you along the meterstick as needed so that the two objects that you are viewing appear just inside one set of notches.
7. For each pair of objects, record the meterstick reading (the distance the paper is away from your face) in the chart.
8. Make sure that you stand in the designated spots for each pair of objects (since the objects are close to us, distance makes a difference).
9. To find the "Angle of Separation," use the nomograph on page 132.
10. Locate the meterstick measurement for a pair of objects on the left side of the nomograph.
11. Use a ruler to draw a straight line from this meterstick reading through whichever size of notch you used to the right line on the nomograph. This number represents the angle of separation.
12. Record the angle of separation in the chart.

Date: _____ Names: _____

OBJECTS	METERSTICK READING	NOTCH SIZE	ANGLE OF SEPARATION
A:			
B:			
C:			
D:			
E:			
F:			

QUESTIONS:

1. How would the following affect your calculated estimate:

a. standing closer to the objects than you should? _____

_____

b. standing farther away from the objects than you should?_____

_____

c. holding the meterstick out away from your face? _____

_____

d. drawing your nomograph line through the wrong (smaller) notch-size mark?_____

_____

e. drawing your nomograph line through the wrong (larger) notch-size mark?_____

_____

2. How can you describe to others where objects in the sky are located? _____

_____

_____

_____

CROSS-STAFF
One per group

A   B

Read
Meterstick
Here

Cut Out

Cut on solid lines.
Fold on dotted lines.

A   B

CROSS-STAFF
One per group

A   B

Read
Meterstick
Here

Cut Out

Cut on solid lines.
Fold on dotted lines.

A   B

131

Date: _____ Names: _____

NOMOGRAPH FOR CROSS-STAFF

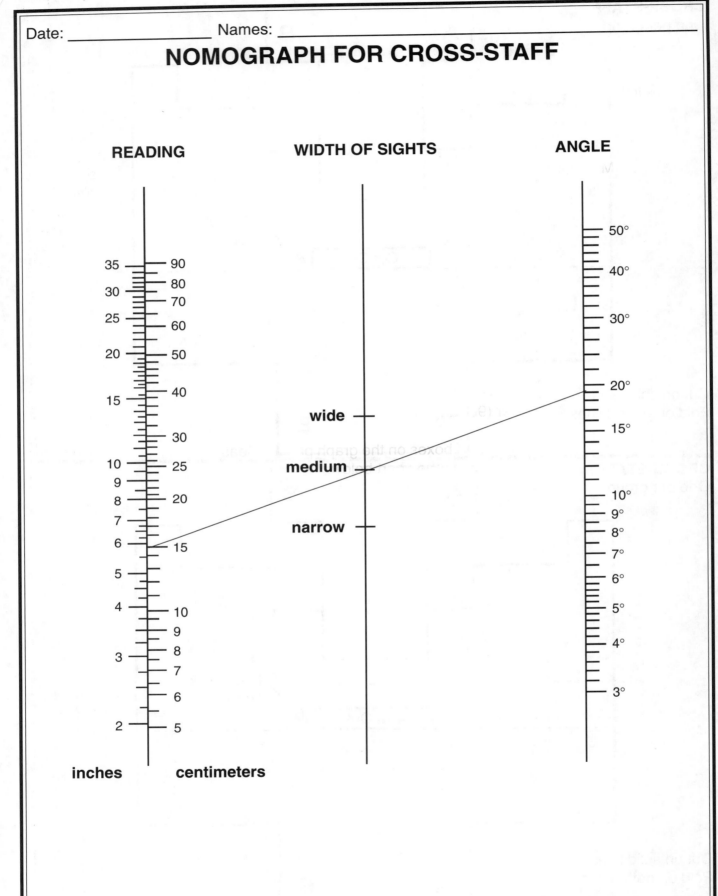

READING

WIDTH OF SIGHTS

ANGLE

inches   centimeters

Date: _____ Names: _____

REASONS FOR THE SEASONS

INTRODUCTION: A survey of Harvard graduates revealed that most of those graduates think that seasons are caused by the earth being closer to or farther from the Sun at different times of the year.

OBJECTIVE: Most people think that we have different seasons because the earth is closer to the Sun in the summer and farther from the sun in the winter. However, at the same time that one hemisphere of the earth has summer, the other hemisphere experiences winter. This would not be possible if seasons were determined by the distance of the earth from the Sun. Actually, seasons are caused by the tilt of the earth on its axis as it rotates (spins) and revolves around the Sun. In this investigation, we will examine the effect of this tilt on energy received by the earth from the Sun.

PROCEDURE:

1. Place a sheet of graph paper on the countertop. This graph paper represents the surface of the earth.

2. Position a flashlight 10 cm above the graph paper so that it shines directly down onto the paper (90° angle).

3. Count the number of boxes on the graph paper at least half covered by the light. Record this number in the chart below.

4. On the bottom half of the graph paper, conduct the following investigation.

5. Position the flashlight 10 cm above the paper and **tilt the light at a 23.5° angle.**

6. Count the number of boxes on the graph paper at least half covered by the light. Record this number in the chart below.

ANGLE   NUMBER OF SQUARES (AREA)

ANGLE	NUMBER OF SQUARES (AREA)
90°	
23.5°	

Date: _____ Names: _____

QUESTIONS:

1. Which angle of the flashlight (sun) lights the greater area? _____

2. If the flashlight (sun) always shines with the same intensity, at which angle would that energy

be spread out more?_____

3. What season would this represent? _____

4. If the flashlight (sun) always shines with the same intensity, at which angle would that energy

be concentrated on a smaller area? _____

5. What season would this represent? _____

6. Think about our flashlight and graph paper exercise, and label the diagram below to show each

of the four seasons for the Northern Hemisphere:

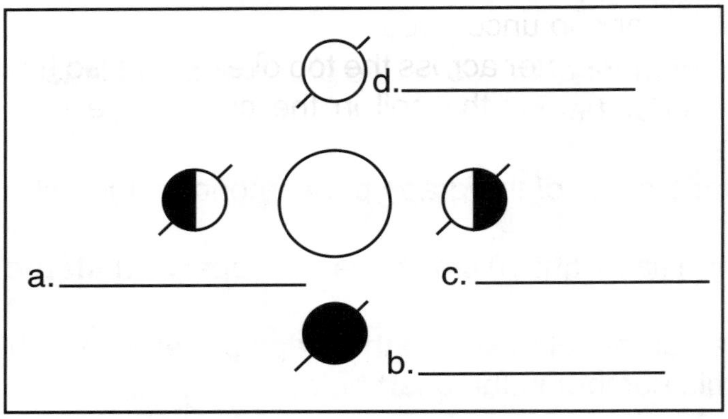

7. How does the tilt of the earth cause us to experience seasons? _____

_____

_____

_____

_____

Date: _____ Names: _____

THE GREENHOUSE EFFECT

INTRODUCTION: If it is 100 degrees outside and you jump into your mom's car, what does it feel like in there? Why is it so much hotter in there than outside?

OBJECTIVE: Carbon dioxide (CO_2) from the burning of fossil fuels and breathing builds up as a layer in the earth's atmosphere. This layer acts like the glass in a greenhouse or the glass in car windows. Visible light passes through the layer, is absorbed by material inside, and reradiated as infrared energy (heat energy) that cannot pass through the carbon dioxide or glass layer. Therefore, the temperature inside the atmosphere builds much like the inside of a greenhouse or car on a hot summer day. Plants are the major removers of CO_2 from the air, but with increased cutting of rainforests and clearing of land for housing developments, we are currently producing far more CO_2 than is being removed from the air. In this activity, we will observe the effects of a layer (like the CO_2 layer of the atmosphere) on heat buildup beneath it.

PROCEDURE:
1. At your lab station you have 2 cups.
2. Fill each about 3/4 full of soil.
3. Cover one with a piece of plastic wrap held in place with a rubber band.
4. Leave the other cup uncovered.
5. Position a thermometer across the top of each cup so that it does not touch either the side of the cup or the soil in the cup. We're interested in change in air temperature.
6. Measure a starting temperature for each cup and record it in the chart below.
7.   a. Place the cups under the light at your lab station if you are working indoors.
        b. Place the cups in direct sunlight if you are working outside.
8. Without removing the thermometers from the cups, record the temperature readings every 2 minutes for 30 minutes.
9. As you gather data, plot the temperatures on the graph provided. Connect the dots that represent the air temperatures over each cup. Construct one with a solid line and the other with a dashed line, and label them "control" and "greenhouse."
10. When you have completed all temperature readings, dump soil back into its original container (shake cup out well), and place all of the cups, plastic wrap, and thermometers back at your lab station.

TEMPERATURES

TIME	CONTROL	GREENHOUSE
Start		
2		
4		
6		
8		
10		
12		
14		

TEMPERATURES

TIME	CONTROL	GREENHOUSE
16		
18		
20		
22		
24		
26		
28		
30		

Date: _____ Names: _____

TEMPERATURE VERSUS TIME

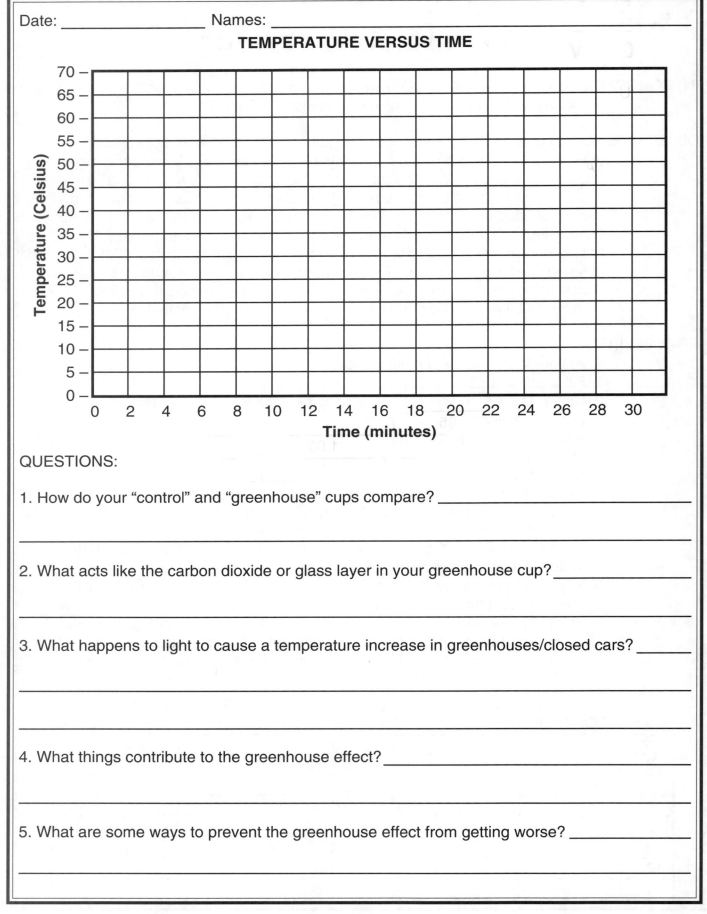

QUESTIONS:

1. How do your "control" and "greenhouse" cups compare? _____

_____

2. What acts like the carbon dioxide or glass layer in your greenhouse cup?_____

_____

3. What happens to light to cause a temperature increase in greenhouses/closed cars? _____

_____

_____

4. What things contribute to the greenhouse effect? _____

_____

5. What are some ways to prevent the greenhouse effect from getting worse? _____

_____

Date: _____ Names:_____

GRAVITY AND ORBITAL VELOCITY OF PLANETS

INTRODUCTION: If a student weighs 100 pounds on Earth, how much would she weigh on the Moon? How fast would you need to swing a bucket of water in order to swing it completely upside-down without spilling it?

OBJECTIVE: All the objects in the universe are attracted to all other objects in the universe by an invisible force called gravity. The distance between the objects and the size of the objects affect the force of gravity between the objects. The force of gravity also influences the orbital velocity of planets (the speed that they must orbit in order to keep from being pulled into the Sun). In this activity, we will examine the relationships between (1) the size of a planet and the force of gravity and (2) orbital velocity of a planet and distance from the Sun.

PROCEDURE:

	SURFACE GRAVITY	DIAMETER	ORBITAL VELOCITY	DISTANCE
Moon	.16	———	———	———
Mercury	.38	.38	1.6	.39
Venus	.95	.91	1.17	.72
Earth	1.00	1.00	1.00	1.00
Mars	.53	.38	.81	1.52
Jupiter	11.19	2.50	.44	5.19
Saturn	9.45	1.07	.33	9.51
Uranus	3.98	.93	.23	19.13
Neptune	3.81	1.20	.18	29.98
Pluto	.24	.03	.16	39.33
Scale to Use	1 = 1 cm	1 = 1 dm	1 = 1 dm	1 = 1 cm

** ALL SIZES/DISTANCES ARE RELATIVE TO THE EARTH.

1. Weigh yourself to find your Earth weight.

2. Students should use the chart of information above to calculate their weights on the Moon and each of the different planets.

(planet weight = Earth weight X relative force of gravity on the planet)

3. Record in the chart on the next page.

Date: _____ Names: _____

WEIGHTS

Student	Earth	Moon	Mercury	Venus	Mars	Jupiter	Saturn	Uranus	Neptune	Pluto
1										
2										
3										

4. Using the data from the first chart and the poster board provided, students should:

   a. create a chart comparing planet sizes to surface gravities.

   b. create a chart comparing planet orbital velocities to distances from the Sun.

5. Note the scales at the bottom of the first chart.

QUESTIONS:

1. How do planet sizes compare to the surface gravities on each one? _____

_____

_____

2. How do planet velocities compare to the distances from the Sun? _____

_____

_____

ASTRONOMY ANSWER KEYS

PLANETARY MOTION (pages 120–122)
I. 1. The shorter the string, the greater the number of revolutions per second.
   2. The closer the planets are to the Sun, the greater the number of revolutions (and the shorter the years are).
   3. You travel faster on the outside of the merry-go-round.
II. 1. As the points move farther apart, the line becomes flatter and more elliptical.
   2. The shape of the orbits of the planets is elliptical, which requires two central points.

LIGHT YEARS AND STUDENT MINUTES (page 123)
1. Both are a distance traveled in a certain length of time.
2. Answer depends on student data. Divide 5,500 by student data average.
3. Answer depends on student data. Multiply student data by 3.
4a. 6:55; b. 6:35, You would be showering.
5. The light that we see reaching the earth has traveled for many years already just to get here. So it is "old" light.

HOW CLOSE IS TOO CLOSE? (page 124)
1. Answer depends on clement zone selected for students to examine—usually a 2–3 degree range around 28–32 degrees Celsius.
2. Answers will vary. This depends on student data.
3a. They are too hot and water evaporates away.
  b. They are too cold and water is all frozen.
4. The farther an object is from the radiant source, the colder the object.

ESTIMATING DISTANCES OF FARAWAY OBJECTS (page 126)
1a. This would produce a smaller meterstick reading that, when multiplied by the constant, would produce a shorter distance.
  b. A fat pencil would have to be pushed farther away from your eye to "just" cover the object. This generates a larger meterstick reading that, when multiplied by the constant, produces a longer distance.
2a. No. The constant is based on the diameter of the pencil that covers the object.
  b. Yes. Anything can be used to cover the object as long as a new constant is calculated.
3. The farther an object is away, the smaller it appears.

ESTIMATING THE ALTITUDE OF OBJECTS (page 128)
1a. A breeze blowing toward you would cause you to tilt the quadrant lower, and you would have to back up farther to do this. Your horizontal distance would be greater, and when it is added to your height, it produces an altitude that is too high.
  b. Opposite of 1a. You tilt higher by walking closer, have a shorter horizontal distance, and shorter altitude.
2. Use a quadrant, and at a 45° angle, add your horizontal distance to your height.

ESTIMATING THE ANGLE OF SEPARATION OF FARAWAY OBJECTS (page 130)

1a. The number of centimeters/inches that the cross-staff is from your face would be smaller, so using the nomograph, the angle would be greater.

b. Opposite of 1a. The number of centimeters/inches is larger, so angle is smaller.

c. Same as 1a.

d. This produces a smaller angle size.

e. This produces a larger angle size.

2. You can describe object locations by using known objects as reference points and describing angles of separation from those points.

REASONS FOR THE SEASONS (page 134)

1. 23.5°

2. 23.5°

3. Winter

4. 90°

5. Summer

6a. Summer; b. Fall; c. Winter; d. Spring

7. The tilt of the earth concentrates or spreads the sunlight that reaches the earth. If the sunlight is concentrated on a small area, we have summer. If it is spread over a larger area, we have winter.

THE GREENHOUSE EFFECT (page 136)

1. The greenhouse cup should be warmer.

2. The plastic wrap

3. Light enters through the plastic/glass/CO_2 layer and is absorbed inside and changed into heat energy that cannot go back through those layers.

4. Anything that adds carbon dioxide to the atmosphere, like burning fossil fuels and breathing.

5. Reduce the burning of fossil fuels and any other reasonable answers.

GRAVITY AND ORBITAL VELOCITY OF PLANETS (page 138)

1. The larger the planet (the greater its mass), the stronger its surface gravity.

2. The farther a planet is from the Sun, the greater its orbital velocity.